Presidential Perspectives on Space Exploration

PRAEGER SERIES IN POLITICAL COMMUNICATION

Robert E. Denton, Jr., General Editor

Listening for a President: A Citizen's Campaign Methodology
Ruth M. Gonchar Brennan and Dan F. Hahn

Presidential Press Conferences: A Critical Approach
Carolyn Smith

Speak No Evil: The Promotional Heritage of Nuclear Risk
Communication
Louis M. Gwin, Jr.

Enacting Political Culture: Rhetorical Transformations of
Liberty Weekend 1986
David E. Procter

Within These Walls: A Study of Communication Between
Presidents and Their Senior Staffs
Patricia D. Witherspoon

Continuity and Change in the Rhetoric of the Moral Majority
David Snowball

Mediated Politics in Two Cultures: Presidential Campaigning
in the United States and France
Lynda Lee Kaid, Jacques Gerstle and Keith R. Sanders

Crime and the American Press
Roy Edward Lotz

A Shining City on a Hill: Ronald Reagan's Economic
Rhetoric, 1951-1989
Amos Kiewe and Davis W. Houck

The Cold War As Rhetoric: The Beginnings, 1945-1950
Lynn B. Hinds and Theodore O. Windt, Jr.

Presidential Perspectives on Space Exploration

Guiding Metaphors from Eisenhower to Bush

Linda T. Krug

Praeger Series in Political Communication

PRAEGER

New York
Westport, Connecticut
London

Library of Congress Cataloging-in-Publication Data

Krug, Linda T.
    Presidential perspectives on space exploration : guiding metaphors
from Eisenhower to Bush / Linda T. Krug.
        p.   cm.—(Praeger series in political communication)
    Includes bibliographical references and index.
    ISBN 0-275-93612-0 (alk. paper)
    1. Astronautics and state—United States—History. I. Title.
II. Series.
    TL789.8.U5K78   1991
    333.9′4′0973—dc20   91-8299

British Library Cataloguing in Publication Data is available.

Library of Congress Catalog Card Number: 91-8299
ISBN: 0-275-93612-0

First published in 1991

Praeger Publishers, One Madison Avenue, New York, NY   10010
An imprint of Greenwood Publishing Group, Inc.

Printed in the United States of America

∞™

The paper used in this book complies with the
Permanent Paper Standard issued by the National
Information Standards Organization (Z39.48-1984).

10 9 8 7 6 5 4 3 2 1

68541

To Sue Lawson

Contents

About the Series

Those of us from the discipline of communication studies have long believed that communication is prior to all other fields of inquiry. In several other forums I have argued that the essence of politics is "talk" or human interaction.[1] Such interaction may be formal or informal, verbal or nonverbal, public or private but it is always persuasive, forcing us consciously or subconsciously to interpret, to evaluate, and to act. Communication is the vehicle for human action.

From this perspective, it is not surprising that Aristotle recognized the natural kinship of politics and communication in his writings *Politics* and *Rhetoric*. In the former, he establishes that humans are "political beings [who] alone of the animals [are] furnished with the faculty of language."[2] And in the latter, he begins his systematic analysis of discourse by proclaiming that "rhetorical study, in its strict sense, is concerned with the modes of persuasion."[3] Thus, it was recognized over two thousand years ago that politics and communication go hand in hand because they are essential parts of human nature.

Back in 1981, Dan Nimmo and Keith Sanders proclaimed that political communication was an emerging field.[4] Although its origin, as noted, dates back centuries, a "self-consciously cross-disciplinary" focus began in the late 1950s. Thousands of books and articles later, colleges and universities offer a variety of graduate and undergraduate coursework in the area in such diverse departments as communication, mass communication, journalism, political science, and sociology.[5] In Nimmo and

Sanders' early assessment, the "key areas of inquiry" included rhetorical analysis, propaganda analysis, attitude change studies, voting studies, government and the news media, functional and systems analyses, technological changes, media technologies, campaign techniques, and research techniques.[6] In a survey of the state of the field in 1983, the same authors and Lynda Kaid found additional, more specific areas of concern such as the presidency, political polls, public opinion, debates, and advertising to name a few.[7] Since the first study, they also noted a shift away from the rather strict behavioral approach.

Today, Dan Nimmo and David Swanson assert that "political communication has developed some identity as a more or less distinct domain of scholarly work."[8] The scope and concerns of the area have further expanded to include critical theories and cultural studies. While there is no precise definition, method, or disciplinary home for the area of inquiry, its primary domain is the role, processes, and effects of communication within the context of politics broadly defined.

In 1985, the editors of *Political Communication Yearbook: 1984* noted that "more things are happening in the study, teaching, and practice of political communication than can be captured within the space limitations of the relatively few publications available."[9] In addition, they argued that the backgrounds of "those involved in the field [are] so varied and pluralist in outlook and approach, . . . it [is] a mistake to adhere slavishly to any set format in shaping the content."[10] And more recently, Swanson and Nimmo called for "ways of overcoming the unhappy consequences of fragmentation within a framework that respects, encourages, and benefits from diverse scholarly commitments, agendas, and approaches."[11]

In agreement with these assessments of the area, and with gentle encouragement, Praeger established in 1988 the series entitled "Praeger Studies in Political Communication." The series is open to all qualitative and quantitative methodologies as well as contemporary and historical studies. The key to characterizing the studies in the series is the focus on communication variables or activities within a political context or dimension. Scholars from the disciplines of communication, history, political science, and sociology have participated in the series.

I am, without shame or modesty, a fan of the series. The joy of serving as its editor is in participating in the dialogue of the field of political communication and in reading the contributors' works. I invite you to join me.

Robert E. Denton, Jr.

NOTES

1. See Robert E. Denton, Jr., *The Symbolic Dimensions of the American Presidency* (Prospect Heights, IL: Waveland Press, 1982); Robert E. Denton, Jr., and Gary Woodward, *Political Communication in America* (New York: Praeger, 1985, Second Edition, 1990); Robert E. Denton, Jr., and Dan Hahn, *Presidential Communication* (New York: Praeger, 1986); and Robert E. Denton, Jr., *The Primetime Presidency of Ronald Reagan* (New York: Praeger, 1988).

2. Aristotle, *The Politics of Aristotle*, trans. Ernest Barker (New York: Oxford University Press, 1970), p. 5.

3. Aristotle, *Rhetoric*, trans. Rhys Roberts (New York: The Modern Library, 1954), p. 22.

4. Dan Nimmo and Keith Sanders, "Introduction: The Emergence of Political Communication as a Field," in *Handbook of Political Communication*, Dan Nimmo and Keith Sanders, eds. (Beverly Hills, CA: Sage, 1981), pp. 11-36.

5. Ibid., p. 15.

6. Ibid., pp. 17-27.

7. Keith Sanders, Lynda Kaid, and Dan Nimmo, eds. *Political Communication Yearbook: 1984* (Carbondale, IL: Southern Illinois University: 1985), pp. 283-308.

8. Dan Nimmo and David Swanson, "The Field of Political Communication: Beyond the Voter Persuasion Paradigm" in *New Directions in Political Communication*, David Swanson and Dan Nimmo, eds. (Beverly Hills, CA: Sage, 1990), p. 8.

9. Sanders, Kaid, and Nimmo, p. xiv.

10. Ibid., p. xiv.

11. Nimmo and Swanson, p. 11.

Series Foreword

Two general social themes that dominated my youth were space travel and Vietnam. My relatives are quick to note that as a young child my response to that perpetual question, "What do you want to do when you grow up?" was "I want to be an astronaut!" While other kids played cowboys or army, I would transform old boxes into spaceships with elaborate control panels and windows. The television series "Star Trek" and "Lost in Space" were mandatory viewing. I was sixteen when Americans landed on the moon. For me, it was one of those special, historical events that you remember where you were and what you were doing when those fuzzy pictures revealed the lunar landscape. Although exciting, for me space travel was never the same after our landing. Although I continued to follow and support the space program with keen interest, my attention turned to domestic issues and more mundane occupations. Perhaps, for me, our nation's historic "mission" as articulated by President Kennedy was accomplished.

I must confess, however, that my childhood joy over and fascination with space travel died with the crew of the U.S. space shuttle Challenger on January 28, 1986. I, like so many Americans, was watching the launch that morning. The flight was special for so many reasons. Perhaps most important was that the flight included our first teacher in space, Christa McAuliffe. School children throughout America were also watching the historic launching. The impact of the disaster for me must have been similar to the impact of Kennedy's assassination on adults in 1963. Instantly I sensed tragedy. With each replay of the explosion, the horror and sadness of the event was magnified. Reagan's five-minute address expressing our collective grief over the tragedy was one of his best and most memorable public speeches.[1] He concluded his brief eulogy:

The crew of the space shuttle Challenger honored us by the manner in which they lived their lives. We will never forget them, nor the last time we saw them—this morning, as they prepared for their journey, and waved good-bye, and "slipped the surly bonds of earth" to "touch the face of God."

I have not watched a live launching of the shuttle since that ill-fated morning.

Presidential Perspectives on Space Exploration is an interesting look at the relationship between how presidents characterize space exploration and the purposes of our space programs. Krug argues that what is most revealing about space exploration rhetoric is its metaphorical quality. Through the use of metaphors, presidents have organized and guided our understanding of space exploration. As a result of reading this volume, I see the parallels between my feelings, reactions, and understanding of space travel during my formative early adult years and the national visions of space exploration provided by our presidents from Eisenhower to Bush.

In addition to providing a wonderful historical overview of presidential perspectives of space exploration, Krug's study reveals the relationships between how we define our space program and how we define the universe and even ourselves. Her analysis also provides insight into the current disarray, or at least disinterest of the public, in our space program.

From a political communication perspective, this study demonstrates the power of metaphor. As the author explains, metaphors can unite contradictory experiences and create a unified perspective. For presidents, they became the primary means of altering our understanding of the space program and merging the concepts of space exploration and space use. Presidential portrayals justify our intentions and provide our motives for space exploration.

Space travel has always held a certain fascination for me. I still retain several mementoes of a youthful visit to Cape Kennedy (now Cape Canaveral). In addition to seeing all the various space movies over the years, ''Star Trek: The Next Generation'' is currently weekly mandatory viewing in my household.

But what of the future of our space program? Can we once again recapture the excitement and genuine sense of purpose of space travel? What we desperately need, according to Linda Krug, is not just a new vision but an appropriate vision of space exploration that will change the current direction of our space program. The blueprint of that vision is clearly revealed in this volume. The appeal, however, may be best expressed in the words of H. G. Wells, carried by Michael Smith, a crew member of the Challenger, on his ill-fated flight into space:

For man, there is no rest and no ending. He must go on-Conquest beyond Conquest. This little planet and its winds and ways, and all the laws of mind and matter that restrain him. Then the planets about him, and, at last out across the immensity to the stars. . . . And when he has conquered all the depths of space and all the mysteries of time—still he will be but beginning.[2]

Robert E. Denton, Jr.

NOTES

1. For an explanation of the creation and delivery of Reagan's address, see Peggy Noonan, *What I Saw at the Revolution* (New York: Random House, 1990), 252-62 and Ronald Reagan, *An American Life: The Autobiography* (New York: Simon and Schuster, 1990), 403-4.

2. As stated in Reagan, p. 404.

Preface

On May 25, 1961, President John F. Kennedy unveiled his plan for a unified space program. He stated, "Now it is time to take longer strides—time for a great new American Enterprise—time for this Nation to take a clearly leading role in space achievement which in many ways may hold the key to our future on earth."[1] Many years later, on the eve of the *Challenger* explosion, Ronald Reagan also talked about the space program. "We've grown used to wonders in this century," he stated. "It's hard to dazzle us. But for 25 years the United States space program has been doing just that. We've grown used to the idea of space and perhaps we forget that we've only just begun. We're still pioneers."[2]

In the twenty-five years separating these statements, American ingenuity and imagination have moved from the science fiction fantasies of space rockets to the reality of space probes, from "Star Trek" to "Star Wars" (the Strategic Defense Initiative), from a great national enterprise to a renewed pioneering spirit. Not only have our physical actions, like launching a shuttle or walking on the moon, made such endeavors possible, so too have our words. Indeed, where America's actions may have failed or proved disappointing, its words have continued to carry the country forward. When the Russians became the first to reach space, Kennedy sought to renew U.S. efforts in the space program: "We have a long way to go in the space race, but this is the new ocean and I believe the U.S. must sail on it."[3] And when the *Challenger* exploded, killing the first civilians to go into space and shocking the nation, Ronald Reagan reminded Americans, "It's all part of taking a chance and expanding man's horizons . . . ; the future doesn't belong to the fainthearted, [it] belongs to the brave."[4] As a symbol-using, symbol misusing, and symbol-making people, our words function not only to impart information but to create images of self and society.

What is most intriguing about words in general, and about this rhetoric of space exploration in particular, is the metaphorical quality. While the popular conceptualization of metaphor is one of rhetorical flourish, "a matter of extraordinary rather than ordinary language," scholarly accounts demonstrate that it is an aspect of language pervasive in every type of discourse.[5] "Sailing on the ocean of space," "the final frontier," the "space pioneers," "exploration for the brave not the fainthearted"— these are not merely flourishes of language but ways of talking about and extending human conceptualizations, knowledge, and life. Metaphor, by its very nature, is the only phenomenon capable of bringing together two disparate experiences (such as pioneers of the West and space exploration) and, in the process, creating a third, unified perspective (space pioneers). Metaphors, then, can open up new ways of thinking about situations and events.

This book investigates the rhetoric of space exploration from a metaphorical perspective. In particular, it focuses on those who have directed the space program—our presidents—and the ways in which their metaphors have organized and guided our understanding of space exploration. As a result, the text speaks to an aspect of the U.S. presidency about which little is known: the relationship between the president, the direction of the space program, and our conceptualizations of who we are as a people and a nation. Consider, for instance, that the category "Directions in Space Exploration" is seldom an entry in texts about individual presidents, and that the heading "Presidential Contributions to the Space Program" is curiously absent from those books that chronicle the space program. Such an omission is clostly, not only for the message it sends about the full range of presidential powers, but for what it implies about the importance of space exploration and science and technology in general.

Understanding the role presidents have played in space exploration is vital to understanding the place of humans in nature and in the universe. National Aeronautics and Space Administration (NASA) historian Eugene Emme has reminded us that our expanding concept of the universe has been a mainspring in human affairs throughout 5,000 years of recorded history.[6] Because it taps into presidential rhetoric and presidential visions, and because it takes a chronological perspective, I believe that this study will reveal what our concept of the universe has been, how it has changed over time, and how it has contributed to an image of who we are as a nation and a people.

This text also seeks to explain the apparent disarray of the U.S. space program. As I looked back over the last thirty years of space exploration rhetoric, many intriguing questions emerged. Why, for instance, was the space program of the 1990s no longer the "fair-haired child" of the 1960s? Why did people no longer flock to see a space launch? Why was legislative support for the space program now so difficult to come by? Why were NASA officials willing to compromise their ethics and beliefs just to make a launch happen? Why was space and space exploration not of national importance anymore?

This book argues that the answers to these questions, at least to some extent, lie in the metaphorical shadows our presidents have cast over the space program. Metaphors are not neutral. They have, in Author Hastings's words, "assumptions at their roots" that lead to particular kinds of action.[7] My guess is that once we had walked on the moon—once we had won the race—we were unable to find another equally compelling way of looking at space exploration. Consider that the role President Kennedy played in the landing of an astronaut on the moon is fairly well known. The recently celebrated twentieth anniversary of that landing repeatedly highlighted the way in which Kennedy rhetorically challenged the nation to enter and win the "race." What we did not see then, however, and what we seldom see now, was footage of Dwight Eisenhower unveiling his "plan," of Richard Nixon ushering in the era of the space shuttle "work horse," of Jimmy Carter arguing for an earth-centered environmental policy, of Ronald Reagan pushing us "to reach for the stars," or of George Bush "taking us to tomorrow." Hopefully, in chronicling the space program and in letting the presidents and their visions of space exploration speak for themselves, clues for a new paradigm of space exploration, or at least some suggestions, will arise.

I am indebted to my parents, Mary Louise and Maurice, for my interest in space exploration. They were, after all, the ones who encouraged me to stay up past my bedtime and watch Neil Armstrong, Buzz Aldrin, and Michael Collins circle, land, and walk on the moon. In particular, it was my father's work with aeronautical design and space research that continuously piqued my interest in space exploration.

My interest in metaphor began while completing my dissertation at the University of Nebraska-Lincoln under the guidance and watchful eyes of Jim Klumpp. Since that time, Bernie Brock and Phyllis Japp have helped me to clarify and sharpen some of my ideas. My department chair, Virginia Katz, was very generous in providing both words of encouragement and research time. My colleagues Howard Martz, Elizabeth Nelson, Jerry Pepper, Mike Sunnafrank, and Debora Petersen-Perlman gave excellent words of support as well. Sue Brockopp, the departmental secretary, did wonders for my morale, as did my Wallyball teammates, the members of my writing group, and all my friends. Finally, my thanks go out to Sue Lawson, whose many words and mini-interventions helped to keep me on track.

NOTES

1. John F. Kennedy, "Special Message to the Congress on Urgent National Needs," 25 May 1961, *Public Papers of the Presidents of the United States, John F. Kennedy, 1961* (Washington, D.C.: U.S. Government Printing Office, 1962), 403.

2. Ronald Reagan, "A Tribute to Seven Heroes's Special Spirit," *Washington Post*, 29 Jan. 1986: A4.

3. John F. Kennedy, quoted in Neil McAleer's *The Omni Space Almanac* (New York: Random House, 1987), 18.

4. Reagan, "A Tribute," A4.

5. George Lakoff and Mark Johnson, *Metaphors We Live By* (Chicago: University of Chicago Press, 1980), 3.

6. Eugene Emme, *A History of Space Flight* (New York: Holt, Rinehart & Winston, 1965), 8.

7. Arthur Hastings, "Metaphor in Rhetoric," *Western Journal of Speech Communication* 34 (1970): 188.

Presidential Perspectives on Space Exploration

Chapter One

Presidential Rhetoric and Metaphoric Action: A Framework

THE RHETORICAL PRESIDENCY REVISITED

In 1981, James Ceaser, Glen Thurow, Jeffrey Tulis, and Joseph Bessette paved the way for a rhetorical interpretation of the modern presidency. Noting that "a week scarcely goes by without at least one major news story devoted to coverage of a radio or tv speech, an address to Congress, a speech to a convention, a press conference, a news release, or some other presidential utterance," they argued that communication has become one of the most prominent, if not the most prominent, feature of presidential governance since the administration of Woodrow Wilson.[1] "What ever doubts Americans may now entertain about the limitations of presidential leadership," they asserted, "they do not consider it unfitting or inappropriate for presidents to attempt to 'move' the public by programmatic speeches that exhort and set forth grand and ennobling views."[2] Indeed, so enamored have modern presidents become with speaking that they and their publics alike increasingly believe that a good leader is one who "consistently exhort[s] in the name of a common purpose and a spirit of idealism."[3] Speaking, Ceaser and his colleagues discovered, no longer merely attends the process of governing, but rather has become synonymous with it.

Ceaser and colleagues were not, of course, the first to articulate a link between rhetoric and presidential governance. Long before "the rhetorical presidency" became a fashionable phrase in discussions of presidential behavior and leadership, Richard Neustadt had asserted that the power of presidents is the "power to persuade,"[4] Doris Graber had argued that "words [are] the basis for official action or inaction, and for the public's feeling of optimism or pessimism, content or discontent, about the course of political life,"[5] and Murray Edelman had suggested that "it is the talk and the response to it that measures political potency."[6]

Political pundits and campaign managers have also commented on the importance and propensity of public discourse. In typical campaign fashion, for instance, Daniel Ogden and Arthur Peterson remarked that

A candidate's image can make him or break him. If he can convince the people that he understands and will respond to their wishes—as Dwight D. Eisenhower and Franklin D. Roosevelt were able to do—he can be unbeatable. If instead he appears aloof and cannot communicate with the citizens, he is headed for defeat.[7]

Even the presidents themselves had already recognized the significance of their own voices. Some four decades earlier, for example, in a speech designed to end the national railroad strike, Harry S Truman asserted that his powers amounted to bringing in people "and persuad[ing] them to do what they ought to do without persuasion."[8] Similarly, in 1979, believing that his presidency was in trouble, Jimmy Carter assembled his advisors for the explicit purpose of "seeking oratory to move an entire nation."[9]

Still, Ceaser and his colleagues were among the first presidential scholars to give rhetoric an elevated role in the institution of the presidency. In their estimation, rhetoric has become more than a tool used by an individual president to accomplish some particular goal; it actually comprises the essence of the modern-day presidency. Changes in the doctrine of presidential leadership, coupled with the rise of the mass media and contemporary methods of political campaigning, has produced the belief that a president is an effective leader only when speaking.[10]

So entrenched has the notion of public discourse become to the modern presidency that it is now virtually impossible to talk about the presidency without also talking about presidential discourse. As a result, increasing numbers of studies of the presidency now address the issue of presidential rhetoric.[11]

THE SIGNIFICANCE OF METAPHOR

In all the discussions about rhetoric and the modern presidency, there is a remarkable absence of talk about the importance of presidential metaphors. Some individual presidents, such as Woodrow Wilson, Lyndon Johnson, Richard Nixon, Gerald Ford, and Ronald Reagan, have been the subject of metaphorical inquiries, but metaphorical activity overall has yet to be tied to the process of governing.[12] A brief review will reveal why.

A Brief History

Metaphor's conceptual heritage is rooted in the *teaching* of rhetoric and public discourse. During antiquity Aristotle, Cicero, and Quintillian—the individuals who first gave form to metaphor—were teachers of rhetoric who were interested in improving the ordinary citizen's ability to persuade the courts of their time. As a result, they were interested in metaphor because of its ability to make language more beautiful and elegant. Thus, for Aristotle, metaphor was a figure of speech designed "to give style, clearness, charm, and distinction as nothing else can" on the basis of a comparison and substitution of "real" meaning for the counterfeit meaning.[13] Cicero was fond of judging metaphor on the basis of how appropriate a comparison it made: "If the resemblance be acknowledged, a metaphor conveys delight; if there is no resemblance, it is condemned."[14] From its very beginning, then, metaphor was little more than the study of a device used by a rhetor to enhance a line of reasoning.

The philosopher-empiricists of the seventeenth and eighteenth centuries solidified this ornamentation view of metaphor with their "substitution" theory of metaphor. The substitution theory argued that metaphor stood as a deviation of natural or normal language and meaning, and thus made sense only when the figurative meaning was replaced with the literal one. Accordingly, saying "We should do something new" was the same thing as saying "We should sail on this new ocean." Indeed, for them, not only was the meaning of the two sentences exactly the same, but the literal translation was better because it relied on "normal" language and meaning.

To this understanding of metaphor, scholars such as Plato, John Locke, and Francis Bacon added a very serious dose of rhetorical misgiving. Beginning at least as early as Plato, philosophers and scientists openly displayed a disdain and suspicion of rhetoric. In the Platonic dialogues there is much evidence suggesting that rhetoric was little more than "persuasion by verbal trickery."[15] In *Gorgias*, for instance, we encounter Socrates' thought that rhetoric is "a shrewd, courageous spirit which is naturally clever at dealing with men."[16] While some evidence also exists in the dialogues, which affirm some importance for rhetoric, by and large it was the dialectical method that Plato saw as important. If dialectic was confined to the realm of philosophical thinking or invention, by contrast, rhetoric was lodged in the realm of stylish persuasion. In that metaphor was considered a figure of speech, it naturally fell into the latter realm.

The disdain for metaphor heightened when these scholars discovered that a literal translation of metaphor resulted in a false statement of fact: We were not, after all, really going to "sail on a new ocean" as Kennedy suggested; we were simply going to try something new. As a result, metaphor became a kind of blasphemy, and efforts were devoted to its eradication. John Locke was foremost in presenting this position; he argued that since metaphors did little except "insinuate wrong ideas, move the passions, and thereby mislead the judgement," they were nothing but "perfect cheats," to be "wholly avoided" in most all discourses. "Where truth and knowledge are concerned," Locke continued, metaphors "cannot but be thought a great fault."[17]

This conceptualization of metaphor held firm until the middle of the twentieth century, when scholars such as Paul Henle, Philip Wheelwright, I. A. Richards, and Max Black began to consider the possibility that metaphor was more than just embellishment.[18] Unlike their traditional counterparts, these contemporary scholars believed that metaphor was capable of capturing something previously uncapturable. They believed that metaphor not only brought together two previously unrelated ideas, but in the process of bringing these two together, created an entirely new idea. They believed that "metaphors could say things." "There is nothing perverse or abusive," Black argued, "in stretching old words to fit new situations. [It] is merely a striking case of the transformation of meaning that is constantly occurring in any living language."[19] Metaphors could, these scholars hypothesized, give us a new way of looking at and thinking about events and situations.

A "New Look"

The line of inquiry that this view of metaphor effected was considerable. From philosophy to English and from psychology to linguistics, scholars began to reevaluate the importance and significance of metaphor. Nowhere was this more true than in the field of speech communication. Working with these new thoughts, critics such as Michael Osborn, Douglas Ehninger, Arthur Hastings, Jane Blankenship, Robert Ivie, Michael Left, and Steve Perry provided a wealth of information about metaphor's nature and function.[20]

We now know, for instance, that metaphor can make arguments, conceal arguments, and become arguments. We recognize that when it is said that *Sally is a block of ice*, the characteristics of *ice* are thrust upon the characteristics of *Sally* such that both Sally and the ice are changed in the process. We realize that the power of a metaphorical image like *economic affliction* resides in our experiences with illness as something that must be treated and in our experiences with the economy as a human entitity. We are aware that metaphors are moral, value-laden, and ideological. We are cognizant that metaphors tap into, exploit, and draw on the various historical, social, and physical resources of the human experience. We know, in other words, that metaphors are powerful moments of reality and powerful invitations to action.

A "New Look" Framework

In keeping in line with these new thoughts about metaphor, in this text I define metaphor as follows: *Metaphor is a linguistic act that functions to constitute, express, exploit, act on, and overcome the contradictions and paradoxes created in a world of humanity's own making*.[21] This definition is not meant to startle the reader anticipating the usual tenor/vehicle or substitution accounting of metaphor. Rather, its goal is to capitalize on a sense of dynamic force and action. It is not as radical as it may initially appear, for like every definition of metaphor, it assumes that what distinguishes metaphor from other phenomena (what makes metaphor "metaphor") is its process of bringing differing things (situations, events, experiences) together.

It does, however, diverge from other definitions in four notable respects. First, it suggests that the action involved in metaphor is one of contextualizing. Second, it argues that these contexualizations lead to an emphasis on drama. Third, it suggests that these dramas come to life via the energy of some dialectic tension. Finally, it purports that this dialectic energy can be divided into at least three additional dialectics. Given the relevance of this definition to the study of the rhetoric of space exploration, I will consider each of these aspects in some detail.

Metaphors Contextualize

Scholars from Aristotle to Kenneth Burke have argued that metaphor involves some sort of categorical confusion, some process of mixing of a thing's given name. Thus, when the label *First Fantasizer*[22] is applied to Ronald Reagan, we are momentarily startled because calling a president a fantasizer confuses our normal concept of presidents. The same is true when the rift between on-the-job mothers and at-home mothers is called a *duel*.[23] Duels are acts that occur between gentlemen with swords, not between mothers with brooms and briefcases.

All too often, however, we fall into the semantic trap of equating the name of an object with the object itself and end up making judgments about the metaphor based on the confusion of categories. That is, we tend to evaluate the metaphor on the basis of how appropriately we believe the merger of categories to be rather than on the insight the merger creates. Consider the statement, *New York City is in Iowa*.[24] Quite literally, the statement is false and rather nonsensical, and yet, as Joseph Gusfield has contended, "When we contemplate the extent of cultural influence across the nation, the statement makes sense."[25] There *is* a bit of New York in Iowa, and "to [rule] it out by strict semantic authority would [be] vandalism."[26]

Burke is even more helpful here; he has noted that our names "embody attitudes" that "prepare us for some functions and against others."[27] William Burch echoed the same theme, stating, "In naming an object there is both a statement as to the texture of the relationships into which it fits and a command as to how one should respond to it."[28] The difference here is critical. To call Reagan the *First Fantasizer* may indeed conjure up an image of an individual given to capricious or whimsical ideas, but more important, it places us into a context in which we have the choice of either praising Reagan as a visionary or criticizing him as a deluded soul. The image is not static but dynamic; it contextualizes us into an action that has already been set in motion. Metaphors are not neutral, Hastings has emphasized, but "have assumptions at their roots" that lead to particular modes of action.[29]

Metaphors Contextualize into Drama

The idea of metaphor as a contextualizing agent becomes even more plausible when we consider the extent to which the proposed definition of metaphor relies on a philosophy of human communicative action rather than human communicative knowledge.[30] According to Burke, symbolic action refers to the encountering and performing of experience (attitudes, intentions, and desires) in language. He acknowledged:

Action requires programs [and] programs require vocabulary. To act wisely, in concert, we must use many words. We must name the friendly or unfriendly functions and relationships in such a way that we are able to do something about them. . . . These names shape our relations with our fellows. They prepare us *for* some functions and *against* others, *for* or *against* the persons representing these functions. The names go further: they suggest *how* you shall be for or against. Call a man a villain, and you have the choice of either attacking or cringing. Call him mistaken, and you invite yourself to attempt setting him right.[31]

A reliance on action, or on the particular ways in which action is enacted within and by metaphor, produces a corresponding reliance on drama; as Burke has reminded us, "When we speak of action we necessarily speak of drama, for drama is the culminative form of action."[32] In this sense, drama is more than a useful metaphor for talking about human action; it is a literal description of what we do in social acts.[33] "Human action is necessarily dramatic," Gusfield asserted. Because "humans use and respond to symbols in creating meanings for themselves and their situations, . . . [c]onflict, purpose and choice are inherent in action as distinct from motion."[34]

Metaphor scholars George Lakoff and Mark Johnson have been equally instructive in enhancing metaphor's dramatic contextualizing essence in their suggestion that Jimmy Carter's stance on the energy crisis took on the "moral equivalent of war":

There was an enemy, a threat to national security which require[d] setting targets, reorganizing priorities, establishing a new chain of command, plotting new strategy, gathering intelligence, marshalling forces, imposing sanctions, calling for sacrifices, and on and on.[35]

Given that metaphors and clusters of metaphors are particularized to a specific situation, we will not find just *any* threat or targets, or just *any* chain of command or new strategy, but a particular kind. Contextualization results in a dramatic setting that, by its very formation, invites certain kinds of actions. Thus, if the proposed definition is on target, it will allow for an understanding of how a metaphorical image like *We must stop piling deficit on top of deficit*[36] commands the American people to "get out of the hole"; it will explain how the metaphor draws on the experiences of piling and the experiences of *money management* to invite participation in a drama of financial responsibility and restraint.

The appeal of metaphor's dramatic action resides in our ability to identify with it; consequently, our ability to identify with the action depends on our ability to compare one situation with another. We must not only be able to "see" a situation in which working women are *dueling* with stay-at-home mothers, we must also be able to "see" one in which they are *not* dueling. That "seeing" process is accomplished via a complex of dialectic forces.

Metaphors Contextualize into a Drama of Dialectic Forces

Without exception, virtually every scholar of metaphor has recognized and spoken of some sort of tension or contradiction inherent in metaphor. However, in spite of such elaborate discussions about "the element of contra-indication," "the metaphoric twist," or the "implied oxymoronic quality," no one has yet made the move from contradiction to dialectics.[37]

The problem is this: While dialectic and contradiction are cut from the same pattern, contradiction alone is unable to establish an epistemic and ontological foundation for metaphor. Contradiction directs attention to what is occurring within the metaphor, while dialectic flags some sort of movement. Recall Burke's statement; for instance, that dialectic does not merely bring together opposites as does contradiction, but functions "to transform any troublesome either-or into a both-and combination."[38] With its stress on being and becoming, dialectic, rather than contradiction, is the preferred idea.

As a dialectically motivated entity, metaphor brings together contradictory situations and attempts a resolution by which the contradictions become acceptable noncontradictions. Metaphors create relationships between incongruous elements of our objectified reality and, because they force a working through of contradiction, they open up new possibilities of dealing with the world. Consider, for instance, Ronald Reagan's assertion, *The MX missile is a peacekeeper.*[39] Here the metaphor reveals war and peace as opposing entities, but also demonstrates how war can be remade into peace. In invoking this metaphor, Reagan brings war into the realm of peace and peace into the realm of war, and thus suggests a restructuring of attitudes toward the MX as a destructive element. The MX remains a war-oriented device, but the metaphor allows its destructive aura to be transcended in the name of peace. If the MX is peaceful, it cannot be destructive.

Yet a second example states the case more clearly. Playing off of a contradiction that argues that government is supposed to watch out for its citizens, a metaphor like *"Our government is asleep at the wheel"* (italics added) aptly captures the tension between the people and the government.[40] What are brought into opposition are not just the literal and figurative meanings nor some tension created by a confusion of proper categories. Rather, here the tension is created by the implicit understanding that our government, as a creation of our social reality, is not doing its job. By dialectic implication, a government that brings us *down* is one that can pull us *up*; the metaphor entertains the possibility of a situation in which government is not lazy, not irresponsible, and not taxing. The metaphor motivates us precisely because of this dialectic possibility and the value (*up* is better) that it activates.

The conceptualization of metaphor presented here is one that takes us from contextualization to drama via dialectics. While one may quibble about whether the contextualization exists prior to the drama or whether the dialectic forces come after the drama is in place, the components need not be separated: The movement is not from contextualization to drama to dialectics, but rather from contextualization to drama through dialectics. Dialectics, then, is the key component in metaphoric action.

Metaphors Contextualize into a Drama of Social, Historical, and Experiential Dialectic Forces

Having established a dramatistic-dialectic foundation for metaphor, it becomes possible to explore the ways in which this dialectic energy manifests itself in metaphorical action. Specifically, the suggestion is that by the power of a social, a historical, and an experiential dialectic, the resources of style, culture, and creativity, respectively, are pulled into metaphoric action.

Conscious or not, the choices of images that a rhetor uses to express an idea embody, to some extent, the beliefs, attitudes, principles, and values of the rhetor and his or her social condition; the act of choosing and invoking a metaphor asserts,

however indirectly, that one should "see the world in my way."
It is here that the social dialectic of identity/identification enters,
for in order to get someone to see the situation from your perspective, you must be able to see the world from theirs.

As we communicate, we perform and proclaim our allegiance
with certain groups and particular institutions; we align ourselves with some sort of sociality. Nonetheless, we make such
identifications, William Rueckert suggests, for the purpose of
building and maintaining individual characters and individual
identities.[41] Thus, there arises a paradox between individuals
and society. We are, on the one hand, unique individuals who
sense and experience environmental stimuli, but those experiences are given form only as we interact with others in the social
sphere. Similarly, it is by virtue of the fact that we have individual experiences that we share with others that we have an
understanding of sociality.

It is the stylistic character of metaphor, which is rooted in a
social dialectic capable of moving us from identity to identification and back again, that reveals character and socializes the
move. That is, in giving form to attitude and expression, the
metaphoric resource of style strategically performs identification
and identity.

Consider the dialectic thrust as it is played out in a metaphoric
passage such as, "For decades we have piled deficit upon
deficit, mortgaging our future and our children's future for the
temporary convenience of the present."[42] Such metaphors as
piling deficit on top of deficit, mortgaging our future, and *temporary
convenience of the present,* are quintessentially Ronald Reagan.
The images draw on experiential and historic linguistic
resources that Reagan shares with others in his culture.
Together, the images project Reagan as a kind of financial hero
bent on enacting the idea of fiscal and moral responsibility.

Reagan's identity as financial advisor stems first from our
experiences of something *stacking up* and the experiences of
money *going down*. The overall experience that is created situates
us in a comparative drama where the "bottom keeps getting
deeper" and the "top keeps getting further away." *Mortgaging
our future* continues to etch out this identity in its suggestion that
we have squandered a decent life, that we have in some way

sold out. In the same vein, *mortgaging* also indicates that in selling out, we have locked ourselves in; mortgages require not only "pledges" but "payments." Given the "no money" situation of deficit, our image of poor money managers becomes a reality.

It is, however, the last metaphor of the passage that solidifies Reagan's advisory image. It draws again from a situation in which poor money management is the key. The *temporary convenience of the present* suggests that the stacking up of our deficits resulted because of our irresponsibility and frivolousness, because we decided to play today instead of saving for tomorrow, and because we chose the easy way out rather than the more difficult but stable route. By dialectic implication, an identification rooted in irresponsibility is one that opens up the possibility of responsibility. In other words, in forging a drama of irresponsibility, these metaphors simultaneously forge a drama of responsibility with Reagan at the helm.

The stylizing character of metaphor emerges, then, in the notion that metaphors strike a social chord every time they are *chosen* by an individual; they introduce an individual attitude while working within a social one. Notice the difference between this approach to the stylistics of metaphor and those of the substitution theorists and the pragmatists. Whereas Aristotle and Searle alike would look at what is expressed *by* a metaphor and ask, "What does it (really) mean?" the perspective developed here would look at what is expressed *in* a metaphor and ask, "What does it do" for the rhetor and his or her audience?

The difference is more than a semantic one. Without the acknowledgment of a dialectic force working back and forth between identity and identification, the first way into metaphor remains focused only on the rhetor and what he or she is trying to say via the metaphor. With the power of a social dialectic, the second way expands the focus to include the individual rhetor and his or her sociality. My suggestion is that because of the dialectic of identity and identification, metaphor individualizes a social attitude; it becomes compelling individually because it is compelling socially.

The historical dialectic divides the situation a bit differently.

Here is a sense of metaphor as a form that sizes up a traditional or universal attitude and that personalizes a given value at a given moment. This dialectic comes to life in the "principle of individuation" or in the idea of the scholastic philosophers that "we may make an intellectual concept of goodness, but we can experience only some particular good thing."[43]

In metaphor, the historic dialectic is revealed in a strategy whereby a universal attitude is remade into an individual one. Consider the way in which the universal image of *the loose thread* was remade into an argument for not "messing with" a woman's right to have an abortion.[44] In his arguments before the Supreme Court, Special Assistant U.S. Attorney General Charles Fried had asked the judges to overturn the *Roe v. Wade* abortion rights decision. He asked the justices to *"pull this one thread."* In response to the *pulling of this one thread*, abortion rights lawyer Frank Susman argued that *loose threads* were a problem. He stated: *"It has always been my personal experience that when I pull a thread my sleeve falls off. There is no stopping"* (italics added).[45]

Here the emotionalism of coming to terms with pulling a thread and losing a sleeve, or even the milder image of pulling a thread and creating a hole, is infused with the emotionalism of losing a basic human right. The image draws on the universal experience of what happens when we pull "just one little thread" and, in doing so, aptly captures the sentiment for what might happen if the Court decided to dismantle the right of a woman to have an abortion. Indeed, the image is a powerful one precisely because it so efficiently reproduces a universal experience. Working back and forth between our universal knowledge of loose threads and the very specific abortion-ruling–loose-thread, the metaphoric image didactically warns that even the slightest pull of a previous Court decision or the smallest rearrangement of a legal document could create a massive hole in the woven fabric of our human rights.

Thus, the cultural character of metaphor emerges in the notion that metaphors have a history that is reproduced and validated every time the metaphor is invoked. Scholars of metaphor examining the cultural dimension were not far from expressing this idea given their suggestion that culture is a substantial part of metaphor because of "habitual use," "liter-alization," and "cultural performance."[46] Without the accompanying idea of a dialectic force, however, their efforts remained concentrated on tracing the etymology of metaphoric names and describing the values appearing in the metaphoric stance. By comparison, owing to the dialectic of cultural form and its individuation, metaphor infuses a sense of emotionalism or value. It keeps us rooted in a historical tradition that also has power at an individual level.

The experiential dialectic emerges specifically in the power of language to open up new possibilities and the recalcitrance of our symbolic and extra-symbolic reality which tempers such free-flowing ingenuity. Black made this point well when he noted:

The rules of our language determine that some expressions must count as metaphors; and a speaker can no more change this than he can legislate that "cow" shall mean the same as "sheep." But we must also recognize that the established rules of language leave wide latitude for individual variation, initiative, and creation.[47]

We can, in other words, "invent" something, but what we invent must tread upon what we already know.

While the experiential dialectic does not allow us to make cow mean sheep, it does allow us to make a cow that is sheep-like. The experiential dialectic pits historical tradition and social fact against individual creativity in such a way that new meaning and understanding arises. Because of the power of language, and in particular the creation of a metaphor, we are able to make new observations, posit intriguing relationships, and, as Burke noted, open up new "cosmological speculations" where none existed before.[48]

Consider an advertisement sponsored by the environmental group Greenpeace. Above a photo of the allegedly drunk captain of the *Exxon Valdez*, a caption reads: *"It wasn't his driving that caused the Alaskan oil spill. It was yours"* (italics added). The text goes on to state that *"the truth is, the spill was caused by a nation drunk on oil. And a Government asleep at the wheel"* italics added).[49] The images contained in the ad are simultaneously recalcitrant and creative. On the one hand, we have a very exacting description of a drinking-and-driving situation; the ad brings together the readily identifiable experiences of driving while intoxicated, passing out or falling asleep at the wheel of the car, and taking a spill. At the same time, however, the ad rearranges some well-known facts about drinking and driving. We come to discover that the one "asleep at the wheel" is not an individual but an entity created to watch out for individuals. In addition, we come to learn that the liquid responsible for the drunken behavior is not alcohol but oil and gasoline.

Thus, what is created here is a new kind of drinking-and-driving situation. The images ask us to think not only about leaving the bar intoxicated but also about leaving the gas station "impaired." They ask us, too, to think not only of the individual who is behind the wheel but also about our government and its policies. Such an ad chides all of us for driving too much and asks us to help get our government off the road of "bad oil policy" before another disastrous oil spill occurs.

The creative dimension of metaphor comes to light, then, with the realization that in its creativity, metaphor is socially and culturally constraining. In its bid to open up, it simultaneously closes down. Scholars of metaphor investigating this dimension were headed in this general direction, as evidenced by the numerous references to metaphor's ability to hide and highlight, to open up and constrain. By ignoring the experiential dialectic rooted in this dimension, however, and by concentrating their efforts on what metaphor *meant* rather than what it *did*, these scholars could only describe the images contained in particular metaphors and, based on that description, venture a statement or two about the constraining images of metaphor.

Metaphoric images, then, come to life in the merger of these various dialectics. While the assumption is that some metaphors (perhaps those we might characterize as excellent) will show shades of all three resources/dialectics, other metaphors (perhaps those we might characterize as okay or mediocre) might well tap into only one or two dialectics. It is entirely possible, for instance, that Ronald Reagan earned the label of "the Great Communicator" because his metaphors tapped so creatively into U.S. history; it could well be that Jimmy Carter will never earn that title because his images failed to invoke the greatness of the American past. While such speculations in general are the subject of a different essay, they are tested here in the arena of space exploration rhetoric.

A METAPHORICAL APPROACH TO SPACE

Overall, metaphors are more advantageously conceptualized not as things but as dialectic dramas of understanding and experience. Calling a *GI Joe* an *"Action Adventure Figure"* (italics added)[50] is not the same as calling it a *Doll;* the understanding created by the image *Action Adventure Figure*, the experiences tapped into, and the dialectics thus energized all lead to the enactment of a very specific drama. The same is true when an executive's wife is characterized not as his *mate* or *partner* but rather as his *trophy.*[51] Here she is cast into the role of prize or reward for his work, and via the image we learn a lot about the executive, his approach toward life and marriage, and the culture in which he lives. Indeed, the same is true when a program of space exploration is called a *race* instead of a *plan*, a *national resource* rather than a *practical benefit*, or even a *conquest of a common frontier* instead of *a step into the future.*

My assumption is that this particular metaphorical approach allows for an assessment of "both the limits and the untapped potential of the metaphorical system guiding the speaker's rhetorical invention."[52] As a result, it will aid in understanding why space exploration thrived so heartily in the 1960s, why it hesitated in the 1970s, why it was renewed in the 1980s, and why it may founder again in the 1990s. More important, this approach will demonstrate *how* these events occurred as well.

The chapters that follow detail each president's metaphorical perspective on space exploration. Chapter 2 brings together Dwight Eisenhower, John Kennedy, and Lyndon Johnson, and explores the ways in which each plays about the edges of a conceptualization of a *space race*. Richard Nixon, Gerald Ford, and Jimmy Carter are joined in the third chapter, as each demonstrates, at least to some extent, an *earthbound* understanding of space. Ronald Reagan's commercialization and militarization of space via the image of *the new frontier* is the subject of

Chapter 4, while Chapter 5 merges Reagan and George Bush in a post-*Challenger pioneer* reconceptualization. Finally, Chapter 6 makes some overall assessments of the various images that have characterized the last thirty years of space exploration, and lays out some advice for the future.

As a final note, in doing this analysis, I drew only on the public speeches and public statements of the presidents. No personal correspondence was evaluated. My assumption is that by giving those speeches and by making those statements, the president implicitly (and explicitly) assumes ownership of the words. Although Peggy Noonan, for example, wrote many of Ronald Reagan's speeches, including his tribute to the individuals killed in the *Challenger* explosion, we give credit for the address to Reagan.

NOTES

1. James W. Ceaser, Glen E. Thurow, Jeffrey Tulis, and Joseph M. Bessette, "The Rise of the Rhetorical Presidency," *Presidential Studies Quarterly* 11 (1981): 159.

2. Ibid.

3. Ibid., 163.

4. Richard E. Neustadt, *Presidential Power* (1960; rpt., New York: John Wiley and Sons, 1980), 26.

5. Doris Graber, "Political Languages," in *Handbook of Political Communication*, ed. Dan D. Nimmo and Keith R. Sanders (Beverly Hills, Calif.: Sage, 1981), 197.

6. Murray Edelman, *The Symbolic Uses of Politics* (Urbana: University of Illinois Press, 1964), 114.

7. Daniel M. Ogden, Jr., and Arthur L. Peterson, *Electing the President* (1964; rpt., San Francisco: Chandler Publishing, 1968), 190.

8. Cited in Godfrey Hodgson, *All Things to All Men* (New York: Simon and Schuster, 1980), 13.

9. This is what the headlines of the *Washington Post* read: "Carter Seeking Oratory to Move an Entire Nation," *Washington Post*, 14 July 1979, 15-16.

10. This position is explored throughout Ceaser, Thurow, Tulis, and Bessette's essay, "The Rise of the Rhetorical Presidency."

11. See, for instance, Robert E. Denton, Jr., and Dan F. Hahn, *Presidential Communication* (New York: Praeger, 1986); Robert E.

Denton, Jr., *The Symbolic Dimensions of the American Presidency* (Prospect Heights, Ill.: Waveland, 1982); Roderick P. Hart, *Verbal Style and the Presidency* (Orlando, Fla.: Academic, 1984); Roderick P. Hart, *The Sound of Leadership* (Chicago: University of Chicago Press, 1987).

12. See, for example, Howard L. Runion, "An Objective Study of the Speech Style of Woodrow Wilson," *Speech Monographs* 3 (1936): 75-94; David Zarefsky, *President Johnson's War on Poverty* (Tuscaloosa: University of Alabama Press, 1986); Hermann G. Stelzner, "The Quest Story and Nixon's November 3, 1969 Address," *Quarterly Journal of Speech* 57 (1971): 163-72; Hermann G. Stelzner, "Ford's War on Inflation: A Metaphor That Did Not Cross," *Communication Monographs* 44 (1977): 284-97; Roger C. Aden, "Entrapment and Escape: Inventional Metaphors in Ronald Reagan's Economic Rhetoric," *The Southern Communication Journal* 54 (1989): 384-400; and Robert L. Ivie, "Speaking 'Common Sense' about the Soviet Threat: Reagan's Rhetorical Stance," *Western Journal of Speech Communication* 48 (1984): 39-50.

13. Aristotle, "Rhetoric," trans. Lane Cooper, in *The Rhetoric of Aristotle* (Englewood Cliffs, N.J.: Prentice, 1932), 187.

14. J. S. Watson, ed. and trans., *Cicero on Oratory and Orators* (Carbondale, Ill.: Southern Illinois University Press, 1970), 237.

15. James L. Golden, Goodwin F. Berquist, and William E. Coleman, *The Rhetoric of Western Thought* 4th ed. (Dubuque, Iowa: Kendall/Hunt, 1989), 19.

16. Plato, *Gorgias*, trans. W. C. Humbold (Indianapolis, Ind.: Bobbs-Merrill/Library of Liberal Arts Press, 1952), 23.

17. John Locke, *Essays Concerning Human Understanding*, A. C. Fraser (New York: Dover, 1973), 34.

18. See, for example, I. A. Richards, *The Philosophy of Rhetoric* (New York: Oxford University Press, 1965); Max Black, *Models and Metaphors: Studies in Language and Philosophy* (Ithaca, N.Y.: Cornell University Press, 1962); Paul Henle, *Language, Thought, and Culture* (Ann Arbor: University of Michigan Press, 1958); and Philip Wheelwright, *Metaphor and Reality* (Bloomington: Indiana University Press, 1962).

19. Black, *Models and Metaphors*, 33n.

20. See, for example, Michael Osborn and Douglas Ehninger, "The Metaphor in Public Address, *Speech Monographs* 29 (1962): 223-34; Michael Osborn, "Archetypal Metaphor in Rhetoric: The Light/Dark Family," *Quarterly Journal of Speech* 53 (1967): 115-26; Edwin Black, "The Second Persona," *Quarterly Journal of Speech* 56 (1970): 109-19; Arthur Hastings, "Metaphor in Rhetoric," *Western Journal of Speech Communication* 34 (1970): 181-93; Jane Blankenship, "The Search for the 1972 Democratic Nomination: A Metaphorical Perspective," in *Rhetoric*

and Communication: Studies in the University of Illinois Tradition, ed. Jane
Blankenship and Hermann G. Stelzner (Urbana: University of Illinois
Press, 1976), 236-60; Vernon J. Jensen, "British Voices on the Eve of the
American Revolution: Trapped by the Family Metaphor," *Quarterly
Journal of Speech* 63 (1977): 43-50; Kathleen Hall Jamieson, "The
Metaphoric Cluster in the Rhetoric of Pope Paul VI and Edmund G.
Brown, Jr.," *Quarterly Journal of Speech* 66 (1980): 51-72; Steven Perry,
"Rhetorical Functions of the Infestation Metaphor in Hitler's Rhetoric,"
Central States Speech Journal 34 (1983): 230; Robert L. Ivie, "Images of
Savagery in American Justifications for War," *Communication Mono-
graphs* 47 (1980): 279-94; Robert L. Ivie; "The Metaphor of Force in
Prowar Discourse: The Case of 1812," *Quarterly Journal of Speech* 68
(1982): 240-53; Robert L. Ivie, "Literalizing the Metaphor of Soviet
Savagery: President Truman's Plain Style," *Southern Speech
Communication Journal* 51 (1986): 91-105; Robert L. Ivie, "Speaking
'Common Sense' about the Soviet Threat: Reagan's Rhetorical Stance,"
Western Journal of Speech Communcation 48 (1984): 39-50; and Michael
Leff, "Topical Invention and Metaphoric Interaction," *Southern Speech
Communication Journal* 48 (1983): 214-29.

21. This definition of metaphor is informed by Lawrence Grossberg's
interpretation of Fredric Jameson's thoughts on dialectic and figurative
language. For a fuller interpretation from a purely dialectic perspective,
see Lawrence Grossberg, "Marxist Dialectics and Rhetorical Criticism,"
Quarterly Journal of Speech 65 (1979): 235-49; and Fredric Jameson,
Marxism and Form: Twentieth-Century Dialectical Theories of Literature
(Princeton: Princeton University Press, 1971).

22. The exact origin of this phase is unknown. For a general
understanding of the term, see Robert Dallek, *Ronald Reagan: The Politics
of Symbolism* (Cambridge, Mass.: Harvard University Press, 1984), esp.
chapter 2.

23. "The Duel between Mothers," *Minneapolis Tribune,* 23 July 1989,
1E.

24. Kenneth Burke, *The Philosophy of Literary Form; Studies in Symbolic
Action* (Baton Rouge: Louisiana State University Press, 1941, 1967;
Berkeley: University of California Press, 1973), 144.

25. Joseph R. Gusfield, "The Bridge over Separated Lands," in *The
Legacy of Kenneth Burke,* ed. Herbert W. Simons and Trevor Melia
(Wisconsin: University of Wisconsin Press, 1989), 33.

26. Burke, *Philosophy of Literary Form,* 144.

27. Kenneth Burke, *Attitudes toward History* (New York: New
Republic, 1937; Los Altos, Calif.: Hermes Publications 1954; Berkeley:
University of California Press, 1984), 4.

28. William R. Burch, Jr., *Daydreams and Nightmares: A Sociological Essay on the American Environment* (New York: Harper, 1971), 12.

29. Arthur Hastings, "Metaphor in Rhetoric," *Western Journal of Speech Communication* 34 (1970): 184.

30. Bruce Gronbeck, "Dramaturgical Theory and Criticism: The State of the Art (or Science)," *Western Journal of Speech Communication* 44 (1980): 315-30. Compare, for instance, the symbolic action theory with that of symbolic interaction. Often termed *dramaturgy*, this approach features actors performing scripts (in language/symbols and behavior) for actors/spectators who interpret the scripts (via their knowledge of cultural rules and significant symbols) to produce social meanings and actions within sociocultural contexts (Gronbeck, "Dramaturgical Theory," 317). There is a performative aspect in the dramaturgical model, but the emphasis is generally placed on the interpretation of these scripts and the knowledge needed, available, discovered, and so forth, for a "correct" performance of the scripts. Thus, knowledge rather than action becomes the controlling perspective. For a more complete understanding of this perspective and citations of scholars adhering to it, see the Gronbeck article.

31. Burke, *Attitudes*, 4.

32. Kenneth Burke, "Dramatism," in *The International Encyclopedia of the Social Sciences*, Vol. 7, ed. David L. Sills (New York: Macmillan, 1968), 448. See also Hugh Dalziel Duncan, *Communication and Social Order* (1972; rpt., London: Oxford University Press, 1970), 5.

33. See, for example, James E. Combs and Michael W. Mansfield, eds., *Drama in Life: The Uses of Communication in Society* (New York: Hastings, 1976), especially xiv-xxx.

34. Gusfield, "Bridge;" 36.

35. George Lakoff and Mark Johnson, *Metaphors We Live By* (Chicago: University of Chicago Press, 1980), 156.

36. Ronald Reagan, "Inaugural Address," *Public Papers of the Presidents, Ronald Reagan, 1981* (Washington, D.C.: U.S. Government Printing Office, 1982), 1.

37. Paul Henle discusses the notion of contra-indication in *Language, Thought, and Culture*, 173-95; Monroe Beardsley discusses the metaphoric twist in "The Metaphysical Twist," *Philosophy and Phenomenological Research* 22 (1962): 293-307; and Paul Campbell discusses oxymorons in "Metaphor and Linguistic Theory," *Quarterly Journal of Speech* 61 (1975): 1-12.

38. Kenneth Burke, "Linguistic Approach to Problems of Education," in *Modern Philosophies and Education: The Fifty-Fourth Year Book of the National Society for the Study of Education*, ed. N. B. Henry (Chicago: University of Chicago Press, 1955), 293.

39. In all his rhetoric discussing the MX missile, Reagan uses the phrase ''the Peacekeeper.''

40. Greenpeace advertisement, *Utne Reader,* Nov./Dec. 1989, 125.

41. William H. Rueckert, *Kenneth Burke and the Drama of Human Relations* (1963; rpt., Minneapolis: University of Minnesota Press, 1983), 42-43.

42. Reagan, ''Inaugural,'' *PPP, RR, 1981,* 1.

43. Burke, *Attitudes,* 47.

44. The case referred to here is the *Webster v. Reproductive Health Services.* The case was billed as the one that would allow the Supreme Court to overturn the first court case giving women the right to have an abortion, *Roe v. Wade.* The Supreme Court heard arguments on the case in May 1989 and rendered its decision in July 1989. The Court chose not ''to pull a loose thread.''

45. ''The Thread and the Cloth,'' *Newsweek,* 8 May 1989, 19-20.

46. See, in particular, Colin Murray Turbayne, *Myth of Metaphor* (1962; rpt., Columbia, S.C.: University of South Carolina Press, 1970), 24-26; Burch, *Daydreams and Nightmares,* 57; and J. Christopher Crocker, ''The Social Functions of Rhetorical Forms,'' ed. J. David Sapir and J. Christopher Crocker in *The Social Uses of Metaphor* (State College, Penn.: University of Pennsylvania Press, 1977), 46.

47. Black, ''Models and Metaphors,'' 29.

48. Kenneth Burke, *Permanence and Change* (1954; rpt., Indianapolis: Bobbs-Merrill, 1965), 258.

49. Greenpeace Advertisement.

50. ''Duty Calls,'' *Minneapolis Star Tribune,* 20 July 1989, ID.

51. Joanne Jacobs, ''Introducing the Trophy Wife and Her Husband,'' *Duluth News Tribune,* 27 Aug. 1989, 10A.

52. Robert Ivie, ''Metaphor and the Rhetorical Invention of Cold War 'Idealists,' '' in *Rhetorical Criticism,* ed. Sonja K. Foss (Prospect Heights, Ill.: Waveland, 1989), 200.

Chapter Two

The Race to Space

In the years prior to 1957, the United States had no formal policy governing the exploration of outer space. A civilian aviation agency, the National Advisory Committee for Aeronautics (NACA), was in operation, but its concern was with airplane design and performance rather than with space capsules. There was also a commitment on the part of the United States to help launch a weather satellite in honor of the International Geophysical Year (IGY), but that too was viewed as an expected contribution to science and the world community and not as an entry point to outer space exploration. Moreover, while the "good" World War II German scientists associated with the U.S. Army and Navy were hard at work designing rocket launchers and power thrusters, their ultimate goal was nuclear deterrence, not the conquest of outer space.

All that changed on October 4, 1957, when the Soviet Union placed a 184-pound satellite into orbit. It was the first in what would become a long list of Soviet "space firsts," and it caused tremendous consternation among U.S. leaders and citizens alike. After all, conventional wisdom said, the United States was the most technologically advanced country in the world; the country with the shiny new automobiles, the latest in household appliances, and the department stores filled to overflowing with the newest mass-produced gadgets. The Soviet Union, on the other hand, was slow and backwards; it was the country with grain shortages, bread lines, and soup kitchens.

Nonetheless, the Soviet Union had put a satellite into space well before the United States.

In the hectic days that characterized the first decade of the Space Age, the United States found itself in the somewhat precarious position of questioning its integrity and character. "How could this be?" and "What can we do?" became two of the most pressing national questions. Committees were formed, congressional hearings were organized, studies were commissioned, and reports were filed. Ultimately, however, it was to the president—first to Dwight Eisenhower, then to John Kennedy, and finally to Lyndon Johnson—that government officials, military leaders, reporters, and citizens alike turned to for answers and guidance on the subject of space.

The type of guidance Presidents Eisenhower, Kennedy, and Johnson each gave to the space program varied significantly. While it is true that the dominant perspective of this time period was that of the "race to space," it is equally true that neither Eisenhower nor Johnson were really keen on waging an outer space contest with the Soviet Union. Eisenhower wanted to put a carefully established and controlled space program in place, and Johnson's concern was with forging a space program that would bring international cooperation and peace. However, the image of the space race prevailed then and still prevails today. This chapter explores the reasons why.

EISENHOWER UNVEILS HIS PLAN

Two weeks after the Soviet Union launched the first *Sputnik* satellite, Eisenhower and his advisors found themselves embroiled in controversy. Nearly everyone in the country believed that the time was ripe for the United States to enter the "Scientific Olympics of the sixties"[1]—everyone, that is, except Eisenhower. To Eisenhower and his staff, the launching of a satellite, even by the Soviet Union, was not a matter of crisis proportion. While it may have been a "neat scientific trick,"[2] a "spectacular achievement that more excite[d] the public imagination than [did] the good, hard, steady work of scientists,"[3] it was clearly nothing to "grow hysterical about."[4] "As far as the satellite itself is concerned," Eisenhower told members of the press at a conference following the launching of *Sputnik I,* "that does not raise my apprehensions, not one iota."[5]

Of course, there were many other things happening in the late 1950s that Eisenhower judged to be more important. The need for a balanced economy and for desegregation, the rise of consumerism and of juvenile delinquency, the decline of science and math skills in students, and the desire to convince the Soviet Union that the United States was working on rockets for peace all dominated Eisenhower's agenda.[6] Nonetheless, in spite of all his other activities, the way in which Eisenhower responded to *Sputnik I* earned him the title of a "do-nothing" president.

In an essay entitled "Defeatism," for instance, Walter Lippmann called Eisenhower "a tired old man who had lost touch with the springs of national vitality."[7] In a longer text, Frank Gibney and George Feldman argued that the administration's response amounted "to one of the sorrier judgments which history can make against an American president and his advisors."[8] In addition, some zealous wordsmith rewrote the lyrics to the president's favorite tune, "Que Sera, Sera" to be more in line with the president's space response: "Whatever will be, will be/The future's not ours to see/Come bury your head with me."[9]

Walter McDougall has argued that "Eisenhower could have avoided these criticisms only by more profligate spending, more centralized direction of R & D, more alarming rhetoric to justify a 'race posture.'"[10] To do so, however, would have been very much out of step with Eisenhower's character and beliefs. Simply put, Eisenhower was a strategist and a planner. As a former general, he was interested in looking at the "bigger picture" and in moving on only after careful study and consideration. Even as the public began to contract "space fever,"[11] Eisenhower steadfastly refused to "mount [his] charger and ride off in all different directions at once."[12] Rather, he stood firm and pushed for a more palatable framework within which to view space exploration activities.

For Eisenhower, that palatable framework is best summed up in terms of the *plan*. Contained in his rhetoric of space exploration are images that juxtapose thoughts about *offense* with notions about *defense,* as well as images that turn *rational knowledge* into *spectacular firsts.* Via such combinations, Eisenhower attempted to convince the American people that space exploration should be looked on as more than a *race.* A cursory look at Eisenhower's space rhetoric bears out this interpretation.

Offense among Defense

Eisenhower's position comes to light in a series of confrontations with the media. When members of the press learned about the launching of *Sputnik I,* they, like many other individuals, were stunned to learn that the Soviet Union had such capabilities. As a result, they talked about the event in terms that made sense to them: those of a race. They asked Eisenhower if he thought that "our scientists had made a mistake in not recognizing that we were, in effect, in a race with Russia."[13] They asked him if his response would be to "bring our program up to par with Russia."[14] They inquired whether the United States' official position was now one of "competing with the Russians."[15] Furthermore, they questioned Eisenhower as to why, given all that had happened, was the country not "moving with a greater sense of urgency to catch up with Russia in the field of space exploration."[16]

Eisenhower did not dodge such questions but rather answered in such a way as to argue that the United States already had a plan of its own in place. "Our satellite program has never been considered as a race; merely an *engagement* on our part";[17] "we have *established* and it has been *published,* at least in *outline,* a *program* of space exploration";[18] "our *plan* is *proper, appropriate,* and *positive*";[19] and "it has been *carefully scheduled*" (italics added).[20]

Proper and *appropriate plan, established in outline form, carefully scheduled*—these are the keys to the kind of space program Eisenhower wanted to establish. Indeed, a *plan* approach to space was the only one that made any sense to him. Time and time again Eisenhower professed to being confused and uncertain about the nature of a space race with the Soviet Union. "Now this statement that we are straddling as far as competition with the Russians is concerned: I don't know exactly what it means," he told Charles Roberts of *Newsweek*. "Our *plan* is a *positive one*, and I see no reason for thinking of it merely as competition with somebody else. It is something we *intend* to do" (italics added).[21]

Four months later Eisenhower again expressed his concern with the *race* image. "I am always a little bit amazed about this business of catching up," he confessed to Merriman Smith of United Press International. "What you want is enough, a thing that is adequate."[22] "You are not," he continued, directing his response to Robert Pierpoint of CBS News, "talking about racing them in finding the particular items or in naming the particular course that you are going to run in this race; you *work out a proper* and an *appropriate plan* of scientific exploration, and you *follow it positively* rather than trying to *follow along behind somebody else*" (italics added).[23]

Here Eisenhower's metaphorical strategy emerges. Centered around a contradiction between offensive strategy and defensive strategy, Eisenhower's images first create the illusion of a nation struggling to stay in step with another country, and then mirror in that image the illusion of a nation taking charge. Consider the way in which a metaphorical image like *following your plan positively rather than trying to follow along behind somebody else* invokes a kind of "follow the leader" or "Simon Says" mentality. As it taps into our experiences with leaders and followers, with the notion of following along behind someone else and giving someone else control over what we do, the image dialectically entertains the possibility that we can shape our own destiny. In other words, it hints that follower and leader are interchangeable positions.

The fact that an offensive, leadership position is preferable is reflected in the way Eisenhower described the first U.S. successes in space. As the United States began to marshall its resources and put its own satellites in orbit, Eisenhower remarked that "these events are the *results* of a *well planned* and *determined attack* on this new field" (italics added).[24] In issuing such a statement, Eisenhower involves us in a scenario in which we become generals on the battlefield working out, incorporating, and reaping the benefits of appropriate battle plans. That Eisenhower thought of our new outer space ventures as fodder for battle is in itself significant. What is more relevant, however, is that in so doing, he could better hone the notion of having a good *plan*.

The way in which Eisenhower established his understanding of a program of outer space exploration is relatively ahistorical. It drew from a common fund of knowledge, but it did not invoke thoughts of U.S. leadership, superiority, or prestige. Rather, it simply suggested that an offensive posture is just as good as a defensive one, and invited us to accept the fact that the United States had such an offensive posture. Eisenhower completed his vision of space exploration by proposing a second cluster of images, which pits psychological firsts against knowledge-based firsts.

Knowledge Becomes Spectacular

In his rhetoric Eisenhower acknowledged that the payoff of a *race* approach to space might be "psychological advantage in world politics"[25] and even increased national prestige. He did, however, view those advantages as inconsequential when compared to the kinds of payoffs a *plan* approach would bring, namely, increased knowledge and understanding. Repeatedly Eisenhower claimed that his approach was the more advantageous one. Upon releasing the Science Advisory Committee's report, *Introduction to Outer Space*,[26] Eisenhower stated, "This statement makes clear the *opportunities* which a developing space technology *can provide to extend* man's *knowledge* of the earth, the solar system, and the universe" (italics added).[27] Upon recommending the creation of a civilian agency to administer the space program, Eisenhower acknowledged, "I am recommending a civilian agency because of the *clear evidence* that space exploration *holds promise of adding* importantly to our *knowledge*" (italics added).[28] Moreover, on August 17, upon releasing a statement about U.S. achievements in space, Eisenhower again argued that "while not one of [our space exploits have] been undertaken solely in an effort to achieve a 'spectacular first' in the eyes of the world, each has *resulted in* just such a '*spectacular first*' in *support* of the *desires* of mankind for *greater knowledge and understanding*" (italics added).[29]

Again, the consistent, positive, offensive movement forward is featured, as are its results: the *promise* of knowledge, *additional knowledge, increased knowledge, greater knowledge.* Against this backdrop the Soviet effort to achieve some momentary spectacular first in the eyes of the world pales. As they physically pull us forward, increasing, adding, growing, and becoming greater, these images hint that we also could move backwards—decreasing, subtracting, and becoming weaker. In the interplay, such images ask us to accept a growth-inducing *plan* posture over a growth-inhibiting *race* one.

The images Eisenhower used in establishing his program of space exploration are not especially startling or overly imaginative, nor do they invoke past and potential greatness. The images of the *plan* were extremely conscientious and consistent, and yet they failed.

Eisenhower's vision of space exploration favored the scientists; his images created a vision of a nation of scientist-generals already hard at work planning how to unlock the secrets of the universe. While Eisenhower was correct in his assessment that the scientists were the keys to understanding space exploration, his vision was weakened by a failure to create an active role for the "ordinary citizen." Indeed, while ordinary soldiers may mill around waiting for the generals to draw up the battle plan, at some point they get the opportunity to put that plan into action. All Eisenhower could offer the average citizen, however, was an observer's position. In his statement on outer space, Eisenhower exclaimed that "every person has the opportunity to *share through understanding* in the adventures which lie ahead" (italics added).[30] Such enlightenment and enhanced understanding, however, were not very satisfying, and at every turn the "average citizen" expressed dismay. This was reflected in the title of a *Newsweek* essay on space events: "They've Got; We Plan."[31]

In all fairness, it is possible that the failure of Eisenhower's vision of outer space exploration resides in his determination to make the program of space exploration a viable national concern. It is possible, in other words, that Eisenhower could not find a way to combine space exploration and space competition without compromising the merits of the space program in the process. Eisenhower was the only president who saw the space program as a viable entity in and of itself. Talking about the program in terms of a *race* suggested that the space program existed for some external reason (i.e., beating the Soviets) rather than for an internal one (i.e., its importance for the nation).

Whatever the reason, Eisenhower simply could not convince enough people that his vision was best for the country and for its program of outer space exploration. Having determined that "the Russian victory in the satellite race proved that the U.S. had not tried hard enough,"[32] the American people went looking for a leader who could mobilize the country to try harder. They found that leader in John Kennedy.

KENNEDY ORCHESTRATES THE RACE

When John Kennedy entered the White House, space exploration was not very high on his personal or political agenda. Indeed, Charles Murray and Catherine Cox have asserted that it was not on his agenda at all.[33] Even though Kennedy had told supporters during his bid for president that "we are in a *strategic race* with the Russians and we have been *losing*" (italics added),[34] he did not produce any program of outer space exploration during his first months in office.

Space became a priority for Kennedy after an ill-conceived and failed attempt to overthrow Fidel Castro of Cuba threatened to destroy both Kennedy's and U.S. credibility in the eyes of the world. Three days after the Bay of Pigs fiasco, Kennedy instructed his vice president, Lyndon Johnson, to determine "whether there is any program now, regardless of cost, which offers us hope of being pioneers in a project[,] . . . which could put us first in any new area."[35] Eight days later, Johnson returned with the answer: "The U.S. can, if it will, firm up its objectives and employ its resources with a reasonable chance of attaining world leadership in space during the decade."[36] Together, Johnson and Kennedy determined that the best shot of attaining U.S. preeminence in space by the end of the decade was to land astronauts on the moon and bring them back. A few days later, Kennedy asked the nation to commit to such a challenge.

In laying out and justifying his goal of outer space exploration, Kennedy used two seemingly contradictory sets of images. On the one hand, Kennedy argued that the United States had to beat the Soviet Union into space in order to prevent tyranny from overshadowing democracy, a move that Richard Fox and T. Jackson Lears have called the image of "jeremiads on the enemy's impending control of the universe."[37] On the other hand, Kennedy also talked about the necessity of prevailing on the new frontier, what Fox and Lears called "exploring the measureless wonders of space."[38] Both goals, however, come together within the overall image of the *race*. Kennedy used this overall image to transform us from a nation of *losers* into a nation of *winners*. Three steps give form to his metaphorical strategy. The first juxtaposes U.S. deficits in terms of Soviet victories; step two reveals the *great American role*; and the third step depicts a free people prevailing on the new frontier of space.

Tyranny 1, Freedom 0

In no uncertain terms, Kennedy acknowledged the grim reality of the score in the race to space. At a news conference in February 1961, Kennedy acknowledged that "the Soviet Union is *ahead* of us in boosters and there is an indication they are *going to be ahead of us for some time* to come"(italics added).[39] Three months later, Kennedy affirmed that "we are *behind* and I am sure that they are *making a concentrated effort to stay ahead*" (italics added).[40] The following month, Kennedy again stated: "We have a *long way to go* in the field of space. We are *behind*. But we are *working hard* and we are *going to increase our effort*" (italics added).[41] Moreover, well into the following year, Kennedy was still giving the score of the space race:

We've *started late*, and we are *trying to* not only—we're *trying to overtake them*, and I think by the end of the decade we will, but we're in for some further periods when we are *going to be behind*. And anybody who attempts to suggest that we're not *behind misleads* the American people (italics added).[42]

Couched between our experiences with *being behind* and *being ahead*, these images bring into play an understanding of a great *struggle*. Working back and forth between *behind* and *ahead*, these images cast us into the runner who has lost ground, the worker whose endeavor is left incomplete and the manager whose agenda is left unmet. At the same time, by dialectical implication, these images suggest that one who is behind can also be ahead; they suggest that in this struggle we can be winners.

It is important to note that what was at hand was not just a *race* but also a *struggle*. Kennedy, in other words, turned our attention away from the competitive process that underlies any ordinary *race* and toward the outcome; he fashioned an attitude of "winner takes all."

What made this struggle so riveting and so enticing was the way in which it became a struggle over character. First, Kennedy defined our character as a nation of people "smarting from a setback." "There is no area," he stated, "where the United States *received a greater setback to its prestige* as the *number one* industrial country in the world than in *being second* in the field of space in the fifties" (italics added).[43]

Simultaneously, Kennedy cast the Soviet Union as a nation on the verge of mind control. He began his address on the nation's "urgent priorities" by saying:

> If we are to *win* the *battle* that is now going on around the world between *freedom* and *tyranny*, the dramatic achievements in space which occurred in recent weeks should have made clear to us all, as did the Sputnik in 1957, the *impact* of this adventure on the *minds* of men everywhere, who are attempting to make a *determination of which road they should* take (italics added).[44]

Here the *struggle* scenario becomes crisper. *Behind* and *ahead* are easily supplanted by *freedom* and *tyranny*; our *setback* becomes an inability to *determine which road* other nations ought to take. The race takes on much more significance; we are asked to join the struggle against the Soviets. A second cluster of metaphoric images which invokes the American character of greatness and leadership helps us to make that commitment.

Playing the Great Role

A number of Kennedy's images contribute to establishing a *proper role* for the United States in the space *race*. Upon presenting the NASA distinguished service medal to astronaut

L. Gordon Cooper, for example, Kennedy said that his administration was "making sure that in this new, great, adventurous
period the Americans are playing their great role, as they have
in the past."[45] In signing a bill making the vice president the
head of the president's space council, Kennedy asserted that it
was "a key step toward moving the United States into its proper
place in the space race."[46] Moreover, upon presenting his plan
for a moon landing, Kennedy argued, "Now it is time to take
longer strides—time for a great new American enterprise—time
for this nation to take a clearly leading role in space achievement."[47]

Kennedy's assertion of our role in space endeavors assumes
greater importance when backed by the force of history. That is,
Kennedy's words tapped into the concrete law of history that
had already determined the greatness of the United States.
During his 1962 State of the Union address, this position became
clear: "Our Nation is commissioned by history to be either an
observer of freedom's failure or the cause of its success."[48] Such
an assertion argues that regardless of which course we choose,
whether it will be a struggle with the Soviet Union or not, we
must at least choose. At the same time, Kennedy appealed to a
different sort of experience to demonstrate that the United
States had no choice but to enter the race: "This Nation has
tossed its cap over the wall of space, and we have no choice but
to follow it."[49]

A longer passage demonstrates the force of historical
precedent. At an address at Rice University in Houston,
Kennedy stated:

Those who came before us made certain that this country rode the first
waves of the industrial revolutions, the first waves of modern
invention, and the first waves of nuclear power, and this generation
does not intend to founder in the backwash of the coming age of space.
We mean to be a part of it—we mean to lead it. For the eyes of the world
now look into space, to the moon and to the planets beyond, and we
have vowed that we shall not see it governed by a hostile flag of
conquest, but by a banner of freedom and peace. Yet, the vows of this
Nation can only be fulfilled if we in this Nation are first, and, therefore,
we intend to be first.[50]

Here again we find the hostile flag of conquest pitted against the banner of freedom and peace, the Soviet Union against the United States. Here too is the belief that we ought to be a part of the race, and moreover that we intend to lead it. Additionally, here is the force of history working to motivate us to accept the challenge. Kennedy's images take us back to all the "firsts" we have experienced in this nation. *Riding the waves* invokes not only the sense that things have been stormy but also that we were able to dominate, master, and conquer those waves. These images motivate us to recreate the past today, not in terms of industry or nuclear power, but in terms of conquests in space.

Prevailing On This New Frontier

The images of the first two clusters include several rewards for accepting the challenge of landing an astronaut on the moon. On the one hand, there is an opportunity to "let freedom ring" and for the United States to "show its stuff." They also provide a way to move from a secondary position into the lead, and to give tribute to the great endeavors that made the country a leader.

Such rewards, it seems, should be enough to complete a vision of a nation reaching for the top. However, Kennedy's rhetoric also offers another reward: the feeling that comes from having undertaken a challenge and an adventure. This reward, however, will not exist unless we make the commitment to the race and to freedom. As Kennedy's challenge unfolds, for example, we are told that we must "pledge that this nation will move forward, with the full speed of freedom, in the exciting adventure of space"[51] and that "we go into space because whatever mankind must undertake, free men must fully share."[52]

The excitement, the challenge, and the adventure are our rewards, all because we made a commitment to the race, to freedom, and, ultimately, to adventure. Two statements give testimony to this image: "We are stand[ing] on the edge of a great new era, filled with both crisis and opportunity, an era to be characterized by achievement and challenge,"[53] Kennedy told the employees of the San Antonio Aerospace Medical Health Center. Similarly, at Rice University he told students:

"Well, space is there, and we're going to climb it, and the moon and the planets are there, and new hopes for knowledge and peace are there. And therefore, as we set sail we ask God's blessing on the most hazardous and dangerous and greatest adventure on which man has ever embarked."[54]

There is no doubt that Kennedy's rhetoric breathed new life into the U.S. program of space exploration. His challenge to put an astronaut on the moon by the end of the decade and bring him home helped to heal a bruised national ego; we were at least going to get the opportunity to show those Soviets what Americans were made of. We would beat them to the moon, we would demonstrate our dominance to sail on this new ocean. As a result, Kennedy became an enduring hero, especially, as Murray and Cox pointed out, to those who worked on the Apollo moon mission.

Twenty-five years after his death, Robert Gilruth [chief operational officer of the American manned space program] would still speak emotionally of how important Kennedy was to the space program and to him personally. Max Faget [head engineer] would still have an embassy-sized official portrait of John Kennedy behind his desk. For Rocco Petrone [head of the Heavy Space Vehicle Systems Office], the decision to go to the moon would still be quintessentially Kennedy, emblematic of the spirit and style of the man.[55]

Kennedy's goal of a lunar landing and overall approach to space exploration, however, ultimately doomed the space program to do precisely what he did not want it to do—to forever "founder in the backwash of the coming age of space."First, Kennedy's *race* posture kept the space program from fitting in comfortably with the rest of our national priorities and commitments. Because Kennedy made the purpose of the space program to demonstrate to the world that we could "master this new environment" rather than to explore space, the program became little more than a means to a political end. As Gibney and Feldman asserted, "When the late John F. Kennedy announced the massive national effort to be first on the moon, he was expressing a political and social instinct; he was not formulating a national goal."[56]

The problem with such a posture was that once the "end" disappeared, the "means" went away. Even Kennedy experienced this phenomenon. Once rumors began to surface that the Soviet Union was not going to try for a lunar landing, Kennedy had to continuously defend his goal as a viable endeavor.

Second, Kennedy made the space program dependent on dramatic and splashy—manned—adventures. Kennedy's manned lunar goal, Fox and Lears suggested, was not the result of a compelling urge not to learn about the solar system but to make a dramatic impression:

As most of the non-defense subsidized scientific community repeatedly stressed, nearly every measurable space objective—in communications, weather monitoring, exploration of the planets, even military reconnaissance—could be achieved far more effectively and at considerably less expense, with automated satellites and probes. Sending men into space was preferable to unmanned projects for only one reason: It vastly enhanced the dramatic impression created by the nation's space exploits.[57]

As a result, the space program has thrived when presidents have imposed Kennedyesque visions, and wallowed when no Kennedyesque vision was to be found. Even Johnson, an individual more committed to the space program than most others, was unable to move the program out from under the image of the *race*. At least for the 1960s, however, the space program thrived.

JOHNSON GOES THE DISTANCE

As president, Lyndon Johnson was not new to the space race at all. In 1957, when the Soviet Sputniks created a national furor, he was the chair of the Senate Space committee and a leading critic of the Eisenhower administration's response. "It is not our technology that has failed, [but] our leadership," Johnson stated in a speech delivered in 1960. "Our national survival could depend upon our being first in the space race and soon. . . . We cannot concede outer space to Communism and hold leadership on earth."[58]

By the time Johnson became president, however, his position

on the space race had softened considerably. "It was really a mistake to regard space exploration as a contest which can be tallied on any box score," he stated during a press conference. "Judgments can be made only by considering all the objects of the two national programs, and they will vary and they will differ."[59]

Several factors accounted for this change in perspective. One, of course, was that the United States was beginning to have successes of its own in space. Alan Shepherd became the first man to stay aloft in a spacecraft, followed by another ride by Virgil Grissom, and then followed by the orbits of John Glenn, M. Scott Carpenter, Wally Schirra, and L. Gordon Cooper. "We were unmistakably behind," Johnson told workers at the NASA manned spacecraft center in Houston; "some prophesied that America would remain behind, that our system had failed, that the brightness of our future had dimmed and would grow darker. But no such prophesies are heard today."[60]

Additionally, for the first time we saw what the earth looked like in its entirety. By virtue of the photographs that the astronauts took in their initial journeys into space, we got an entirely new vantage point. That such photos impacted on Johnson's rhetoric seems apparent. Gone was the stark polarity between the Soviets and the United States, gone was the "us against them" mentality so prevalent in Kennedy's rhetoric, and gone was the struggle. In their place stood a vision that bound rather than separated, an understanding of a nation working together to conquer a common frontier. (This was almost the case, at least.) While Johnson's images went a long way in restructuring our understanding of space and the space race, they were not quite able to overcome remnants of the old perspective. There was, in other words, a significant contradiction in Johnson's rhetoric that was not resolved.

Walking Together Toward Peace

Johnson's images seem inviting. They carry forth the ideals of *peace* and *peaceful exploration* linked with *commonality, unity,* and *humanity.* Where before we were struggling with the Soviet Union over control of the universe, now we were working with them for the common good. Consider some passages in which Johnson demonstrated the extent of this merger: "The Soviet accomplishment and our own scheduled efforts demonstrate, I think, dramatically and convincingly the important role that man himself will play in the exploration of the space frontier,"[61] Johnson stated at a March 1965 news conference. Several months later, his rhetoric echoed the same cooperative theme: "As [man] draws nearer to the stars, why should he not also draw nearer to his neighbor? As we push even more deeply into the universe, we must constantly learn to cooperate across the frontiers that really divide earth's surface."[62]

Following a flight by astronauts Jim McDivitt and Ed White, Johnson confessed, "We hope and we do pray that the time will come when all men of all nations will join together to explore space together, and walk side by side toward peace."[63] Moreover, during a talk with employees at the NASA center in Houston, he said, "We of America invite you [people of communist countries] to open your curtains, come through the doorways and the walls that you have built, and join with us to walk together toward peace for all people."[64] Another similar statement of Johnson's was, "Pull back the curtains, come through the walls, join hands in common cause, take a great walk together toward peace. We have no need for arms races or moon races."[65] While the similarity of these statements is intriguing in and of itself, what is more riveting is the overall sense of cooperation they ignite. That cooperation is forged first as the images draw on a previous understanding of the "space race" and history of the cold war. We are asked to look beyond the struggle of a previous time and to look forward to new relationships.

The images work back and forth between an understanding of unity and division in nations' assertions of their strength. The image of the *curtain* and the *wall* make clear inferences about the Iron Curtain, the Berlin Wall, and the Wall of China—all of which impose themselves on human relationships. The images suggest that even though dividers exist between people, it is possible for unity to occur. Of course, a breaking of those dividers must come about, which can happen if people throughout the world realize the commonality of their mission in space.

At the same time, these images become powerful motivaters

because of the way in which they play on our physical experiences with joining hands, sliding back curtains, opening doors, meeting other people, and coming out from behind some sort of barrier. The images tap into a sort of "Wizard of Oz" mentality— at first, the "all and powerful Oz" loomed large and fearful, yet after the curtain was pulled away we learn that he is really a "nice guy." These images invite us to go beyond the divisions and toward unity. Moreover, the unity begins to take hold because of the commonality that Johnson argues exists between all people of the world: space.

Conquering the Common Frontier Together

In Kennedy's vision of space, outer space represented an arena whereby *freedom* could triumph over *tyranny*, where the United States could reign victorious over the Soviet Union. His vision sought to divide the world or, more appropriately, to instill a sense of division between the United States and the Soviet Union. In Johnson's vision, the division began to change into unity. It did so via the image of conquering the ultimate frontier. Here, the arena of space becomes the enemy against which all other nations must pit themselves.

To achieve his aim, Johnson slipped into the language of war to get across his plan of peace. "Space is the only form of *conquest* in which modern man can *proudly* and *profitably engage*. In this *struggle all* men are *allies*, and the only *enemy* is a *hostile environment*. The *victory* over this final enemy will *belong* not just to Americans but *to all* the world."[66] "The true significance of space is the story of *victory over the forces of nature*" (italics added).[67]

Here, then, is what ought to motivate our coming together: the hostile medium of space. Such thoughts ask everyone to turn away from their earlier divisions and to look skyward, and, in the process, to realize that on earth we stand together as one people. The images of war that back these thoughts take on additional significance against the backdrop of the Vietnam War. Here, Johnson asserted, is a struggle that assures victory for all; here is one that engenders pride and will render itself cost-effective. We are asked, in other words, to make a comparison between the war on earth and the potential war in space, and to realize the advantages of turning our sights to space.

Standing Ground

Johnson's images offer a very inviting perspective toward space; they bring back the notion that space exploration is profitable (albeit in terms of a war), and bring home the fact that it is an adventure that belongs to everyone. This vision, however, is marred by remnants of the old space perspective—the race/struggle. Even as Johnson asks for cooperation, he argues for continued competition. Even as he stresses peace, he invites war. The intensity of the race/struggle is lessened, but it is present nonetheless.

Upon accepting the Robert H. Goddard trophy for action in the area of space, Johnson stated:

I want to declare once again that so long as I am in public office, I am going to do everything within my power and my capability to prevent us from falling behind. We intend to land the first man on the surface of the moon and we intend to do this in the decade of the sixties.[68]

The only difference between this statement and those of Kennedy is that Johnson took personal responsibility for making sure that the United States did not fall behind. Whereas Kennedy put the onus of responsibility for the *race* on history and on our ability to accept this challenge, Johnson invited us to rely on him as the one who would safeguard our program.

Such personal assurances, however, do not detract from the impact of the remaining *race* images. After inspecting the space facilities at Cape Kennedy, for instance, Johnson stated, "We cannot be the leaders of the world and the follower in space."[69] Johnson admitted, "We haven't wiped out all of the deficiencies in our program yet, but we have caught up and we are pulling ahead."[70] Moreover, upon signing a bill authorizing new appropriations for NASA, Johnson remarked: "The period ahead will bring continued strong competition for space leadership. We are well prepared for that."[71]

There is no doubt that the type of competition Johnson's rhetoric alludes to here is more friendly than the kind of struggle Kennedy depicted. Still, what is put forth is the commitment to be the leader, to be first. Moreover, if there is any question about Johnson's position, a passage from a speech given after inspecting NASA's Michoud assembly facility near New Orleans sets the record straight. Again using the language of war, Johnson divided the world once again: "Today we stand at the gateway to another and more glorious new world. We will never surrender our station. We will not abandon our dream. We will never evacuate the frontiers of space. We must be the space pioneers who lead the way to the stars."[72] Thus, what Johnson gave with the right hand, he here took back with the left. Thoughts of joining all humanity have no place in this vision of standing our ground and making our claims.

Johnson's contradictory vision of the space program did not help its acceptance or give it the kind of solid foundation it needed. Indeed, like Kennedy, Johnson, was unable to get the nation to commit to his extensive program of space exploration. Perhaps, as his contradictory images demonstrate, Johnson too was pulled in different directions. For instance, as much as Johnson wanted an American to go to the moon, he wanted even more to erect his "Great Society." In the process of attaining this society, however, he revealed to everyone that even amidst great wealth—and the United States indeed was a land of great wealth—there was much poverty. Thus, rather than being able to move us forward together, his policies and images served to further divide us.

The same was true with his perspective on the Vietnam War. As much as Johnson wanted the war to end, he kept sending the troops and the bombers. Rather than uniting the country and countries around the world, such decisions served to pit people against each other.

Both the Great Society and the war prevented many people from achieving a unified perspective on the subject of space. The Great Society was an expensive proposition, as was the war. As a result, questions were raised about the necessity of spending large sums of money in space when there was such a need for it on earth. Consequently, there really was no national commitment on a program of outer space exploration.

Historian Vaughn Bornet has agreed, stating:

Because many people during the 1960s had not sought and were not sold on the ultimate value of the man-on-the-moon effort, the giant strides in space technology—which were really analogous to the earlier

Manhattan project or the Marshall Plan in ultimate payoff—were not evaluated by masses of contemporaries as a genuine revolution in human history.[73]

As a result, our "great" program of space exploration, like Johnson, came to the end of the 1960s in a state of crisis and disarray. A new vision would be needed to alter our perspective.

NOTES

1. Simon Ramo, executive vice-president of the Thompson-Ramo-Wooldridge Corporation; quoted in Donald W. Cox, *The Space Race* (Philadelphia: Chilton Books, 1962), 145.

2. Defense Secretary Charles Wilson; quoted in Walter A. McDougall, . . . *The Heavens and the Earth: A Political History of the Space Age* (New York: Basic Books, 1985), 146.

3. Dwight D. Eisenhower, "News Conference," 26 Jan. 1960, *Public Papers of the Presidents of the United States, Dwight D. Eisenhower, 1960-61* (Washington, D.C.: U.S. Government Printing Office, 1961). (Hereafter referred to as *PPP, DDE, year*).

4. Dwight D. Eisenhower, "News Conference," 9 Oct. 1957, *PPP, DDE, 1957* (Washington, D.C.: U.S. Government Printing Office, 1958), 728.

5. Eisenhower, "News Conference," 9 Oct. 1957, 730.

6. See, for example, McDougall, *Heavens*, 141-237; and Cox, *Space Race*, 133-47.

7. Quoted in Cox, *Space Race*, 137.

8. Frank B. Gibney and George J. Feldman, *The Reluctant Space-Farers: A Study in the Politics of Discovery* (New York: NAL-World, 1965), 28.

9. Quoted in Cox, *Space Race*, 50.

10. McDougall, *Heavens*, 126.

11. Richard W. Fox and T. Jackson Lears, eds. *The Culture of Consumption* (New York: Pantheon, 1983), 192.

12. Dwight D. Eisenhower, "Radio and Television Address to the American People on Science in National Security," 7 Nov. 1957, *PPP, DDE, 1957*, 798.

13. Eisenhower, "News Conference," 9 Oct. 1957, *PPP, DDE, 1957*, 722.

14. "The Nation," *Newsweek* 14 Oct. 1957, 41.

15. Dwight D. Eisenhower, "News Conference," 22 Oct. 1959, *PPP, DDE, 1959* (Washington, D.C.: U.S. Government Printing Office, 1960), 733.

16. Eisenhower, "News Conference," 26 Jan. 1960, *PPP, DDE, 1960-61,* 127.

17. Eisenhower, "News Conference," 9 Oct. 1957, *PPP, DDE, 1957,* 719.

18. Eisenhower, "News Conference" 22 Oct. 1959, *PPP, DDE, 1959,* 734.

19. "News Conference," 3 Feb. 1960, *PPP, DDE, 1960-61,* 146.

20. Dwight D. Eisenhower, "Statement by the President Summarizing Facts in the Development of an Earth Satellite by the United States," 9 Oct. 1957, *PPP, DDE, 1957,* 735.

21. "News Conference," 22 Oct. 1959, *PPP, DDE, 1959,* 734.

22. "News Conference," 3 Feb. 1960, *PPP, DDE, 1960-61,* 145.

23. "News Conference," 3 Feb. 1960, *PPP, DDE, 1960-61,* 146.

24. Dwight D. Eisenhower, "Statement by the President on United States' Achievements in Space," 17 Aug. 1960, *PPP, DDE, 1960-61,* 644.

25. Eisenhower, "News Conference," 9 Oct. 1957, *PPP, DDE, 1957,* 723.

26. "Advisory Committee Reports on 'Introduction to Outer Space," *Congressional Quarterly,* 4 Ap. 1958, 421-24.

27. Dwight D. Eisenhower, "Statement by the President on the Release of the Science Advisory Committee's 'Introduction to Outer Space,'" 26 Mar. 1958, *PPP, DDE, 1958* (Washington, D.C.: U.S. Government Printing Office, 1959), 58.

28. Dwight D. Eisenhower, "Statement on the Proposing of the National Aeronautic and Space Agency," 14 May 1958, *PPP, DDE, 1958,* 407.

29. Eisenhower, "Achievements in Space," 17 Aug. 1960, *PPP, DDE, 1960-61,* 644.

30. Eisenhower, "Introduction to Outer Space," *PPP, DDE, 1958,* 57.

31. "The Nation," *Newsweek,* 14 Oct. 1957, 38.

32. *Time,* 14 Oct. 1957, 28.

33. Charles Murray and Catherine Bly Cox, *Apollo* (New York: Simon and Schuster, 1989), 60.

34. John F. Kennedy, "Campaign Address," 10 Oct. 1960; quoted in Paul Stares, *The Militarization of Space* (Ithaca, N.Y.: Cornell University Press, 1985), 72.

35. John F. Kennedy, "News Conference," 12 April 1961, *Public Papers of the Presidents of the United States, John F. Kennedy, 1961* (Washington, D.C.: U.S. Government Printing Office, 1962), 310. (Hereafter abbreviated *PPP, JFK, year*).

36. Vaughn Davis Bornet, *The Presidency of Lyndon B. Johnson* (Lawrence, Kansas: University of Kansas Press, 1983), 214.

37. Fox and Lears, *Culture of Consumption*, 195.

38. Ibid.

39. John F. Kennedy, "News Conference," 15 Feb. 1961, *PPP, JFK, 1961*, 95.

40. Kennedy, "News Conference," 12 April 1961, *PPP, JFK, 1961*, 263.

41. John F. Kennedy, "News Conference," 5 May 1961, *PPP, JFK, 1961*, 358.

42. John F. Kennedy, "News Conference," 22 Aug. 1962, *PPP, JFK, 1962* (Washington, D.C.: U.S. Government Printing Office, 1963), 633.

43. John F. Kennedy, "Address in Los Angeles at a Dinner of the Democratic Party of California," 18 Nov. 1961, *PPP, JFK, 1961*, 734.

44. John F. Kennedy, "Special Message to the Congress on Urgent National Needs," 25 May 1961, *PPP, JFK, 1961*, 403.

45. John F. Kennedy, "Remarks upon Presenting the NASA Distinguished Service Medal to Astronaut Cooper," 21 May 1963, *PPP, JFK, 1963* (Washington, D.C.: U.S. Government Printing Office, 1964), 417.

46. John F. Kennedy, "Statement by the President Upon Signing A Bill Amending the Aeronautics and Space Act," 25 April 1961, *PPP, JFK, 1961*, 321-22.

47. Kennedy, "Urgent National Needs," *PPP, JFK, 1961*, 403.

48. John F. Kennedy, "State of the Union Address," 11 Jan. 1962, *PPP, JFK, 1962*, 5.

49. John F. Kennedy, "Remarks in San Antonio at the Dedication of the Aerospace Medical Health Center," 21 Nov. 1963, *PPP, JFK, 1963*, 883.

50. John F. Kennedy, "Address at Rice University in Houston Texas, 12 Sept. 1962, *PPP, JFK, 1962*, 669.

51. Kennedy, "Urgent National Needs," *PPP, JFK, 1961*, 405.

52. Kennedy, "Urgent National Needs," *PPP, JFK, 1961*, 404.

53. Kennedy, "Remarks in San Antonio," *PPP, JFK, 1963*, 882.

54. Kennedy, "Address at Rice University, *PPP, JFK, 1962*, 671.

55. Murray and Cox, *Apollo*, 60-61.

56. Gibney and Feldman, *Space-Farers*, 128.

57. Fox and Lears, *Culture of Consumption*, 194.

58. Lyndon B. Johnson, quoted in Cox, *Space Race*, 51.

59. Lyndon B. Johnson, "News Conference," 20 Mar. 1965, *Public Papers of the Presidents of the United States, Lyndon B. Johnson, 1965*, vol. I (Washington, D.C.: U.S. Government Printing Office, 1966), 306. (Hereafter abbreviated, *PPP, LBJ, year*).

60. Lyndon B. Johnson, "Remarks in Houston at the NASA Manned Spacecraft Center," 11 June 1965, *PPP, LBJ, 1965,* vol. II (Washington, D.C.: U.S. Government Printing Office, 1966), 656.

61. Johnson, "News Conference," 20 Mar. 1965, *PPP, LBJ, 1965,* I:306.

62. Lyndon B. Johnson, "News Conference," 29 Aug. 1965, *PPP, LBJ, 1965,* II: 945.

63. Lyndon B. Johnson, "Telephone Conversation Between the President and Astronauts McDivitt and White, 7 June 1965, *PPP, LBJ, 1965,* II: 646.

64. Lyndon B. Johnson, "Remarks in Houston at the NASA Manned Spacecraft Center," 11 June 1965, *PPP, LBJ, 1965,* II: 656.

65. Lyndon B. Johnson, "Remarks at a Ceremony in the State Department Auditorium in Honor of the Gemini 4 Astronauts," 17 June 1965, *PPP, LBJ, 1965,* II: 685.

66. Lyndon B. Johnson, "Statement by the President on the Flight of Gemini 7," 4 Dec. 1965, *PPP, LBJ, 1965,* II: 1135.

67. Lyndon B. Johnson, "Remarks Upon Accepting the Robert H. Goddard Trophy," 16 Mar. 1966, *PPP, LBJ, 1966,* vol. I (Washington, D.C.: U.S. Government Printing Office, 1967), 330.

68. Ibid.

69. Lyndon B. Johnson, "Remarks After Inspecting Space Facilities at Cape Kennedy, 15 Sept. 1964, *PPP, LBJ, 1963-64,* vol. II (Washington, D.C.: U.S. Government Printing Office, 1965), 1071.

70. Johnson, "Accepting Goddard Trophy," I: 330.

71. Lyndon B. Johnson, "Statement by the President Upon Signing a Bill Authorizing Appropriations for NASA," 5 Aug. 1966, *PPP, LBJ, 1966,* II: 802.

72. Lyndon B. Johnson, "Speech Given Following an Inspection of NASA's Michoud Assembly Facility near New Orleans," 12 Dec. 1967, *PPP, LBJ, 1967,* vol. II (Washington, D.C.: U.S. Government Printing Office, 1968), 1124.

73. Bornet, *The Presidency of Lyndon B. Johnson,* 348.

Chapter Three

Routinizing Space

On July 20, 1969, Neil Armstrong unlocked the latch that bolted
the door of his lunar module, *Eagle*, and became the first human
to set foot upon alien soil. It had taken eight and a quarter years
of hard work and commitment, but the United States had finally
lived up to Kennedy's challenge. We had demonstrated our
superiority in space; we had won the space race.

Headlines across the country and around the world proclaimed our victory. Howard Benedict, a long-time observer of
space events, wrote: "In London's Trafalgar Square, crowds
screamed and applauded. In New York's Yankee Stadium, the
baseball scoreboard flashed 'They're on the Moon!' The stadium
was filled with cheers, then there was a moment of silence
before the 35,000 fans sang 'American the Beautiful.'"[1] Celebra-
tions were held, ticker-tape parades commenced, and medal-
pinnings, hand-shaking, and back-slapping were the order of
the day.

Then it was over. As the tide of enthusiasm for *Apollo 11* began
to wane, support for the space program dwindled. We went
back to the moon five more times. We put the *Skylab* work-
station into orbit and sent three consecutive crews to live and
work in it for months at a time. We even docked with a Soviet
spacecraft in orbit and shared an evening's meal. However,
what remained in our collective consciousness was the *Eagle*,
Neil Armstrong, and his statement, "One small step for man,
one giant leap for mankind."

That the remaining events concerning Apollo appear fuzzy in
our memories is a tribute to the metaphorical perspective forged

during the 1970s. With the space race behind us, Presidents Richard Nixon, Gerald Ford, and Jimmy Carter all turned their sights on a different understanding of space exploration. In different ways and with differing emphases, each worked to move us beyond the exploration stage and toward the utilization stage. While the space exploits of the 1960s were considered to be awe-inspiring events, those of the 1970s were intentionally called ordinary and routine. Unfortunately, in taking the special quality out of space events, and in making space a part of our everyday lives, our program of space exploration was cast into mediocrity. This chapter explains how this came about.

NIXON COMMANDEERS A SPACE TRUCK

Richard Nixon, like Lyndon Johnson, was not new to the space program or to the politics of space. He was at Eisenhower's side when the news of *Sputnik I* splashed across the front page of every paper in the nation. He was the first member of Eisenhower's administration to speak out about the Soviet launch, warning that "we could make no greater mistake than to brush off [*Sputnik I*] as a scientific stunt of more significance to the man in the moon than to men on earth."[2]

However, the Apollo program that Nixon inherited from Lyndon Johnson in 1969 was very different from the one Johnson had inherited from Kennedy or that Kennedy had gotten from Eisenhower. In the twelve years separating Nixon's 1957 speech on the Soviet "stunt" and his 1969 earth-to-moon phone call with Neil Armstrong, the world had changed dramatically. Where before Americans had felt excitement about the prospects of space, now there was only apathy and boredom. Where once there had been images of technological marvels in space, now there were images of technological failures on earth. Where once there "was Camelot, now there was My Lai, Watts, Tet, Dallas, and Chicago."[3]

With sentiment against the space program running high, Nixon could no longer invoke what had become known as the Columbus Principle; Nixon could not argue, as had those before him, that "curiosity and purposefulness were the only prerequisites in space exploration" or that space exploration could continue without any "palpable justifications."[4] Nor could Nixon reasonably speak of the "Soviet threat" in space. While the Soviet Union was continuing to aggressively pursue its space program, the United States had already proven its superiority. According to the rules of the space race set up by Kennedy in 1961, the United States had already won.

Amidst domestic strife and moral disillusionment, Nixon had to create a new identity for space exploration. A close look at Nixon's rhetoric reveals a strategy designed to do just that. Nixon crafted a philosophy of pragmatism out of a philosophy of wonderment. Nixon did not ask the American people to give up space exploration for domestic concerns, but rather, in the spirit of metaphoric transfer, demonstrated how the foundation of wonderment and the foundation of pragmatism were one and the same. Indeed, the unique character of Nixon's rhetoric lies in the way in which he juxtaposed the discovery of space with the discovery of earth, the manner in which he combined the necessity of space exploration with the search for our roots, and finally, the fashion in which he transformed space exploration into an everyday occurrence. In other words, Nixon crafted a space program for the future based on current earthly priorities.

The Heavens among the Earth

Nixon worked from the very beginning to not only take us back into space but also to turn us homeward. His metaphors established an image of people looking out into the galaxy and, from the galaxy, back to earth. A quick glance through Nixon's speeches reveals metaphorical images such as: *"reaching with precision for the moon* and *falling into raucous discord on earth"*;[5] *"in throwing wide the horizons of space we have discovered new horizons on earth"*;[6] *"in that moment of surpassing technological triumph, men turned their thoughts toward home and humanity"*;[7] *"however far we reach, our destiny lies not in the stars but on earth"*;[8] *"technological genius but human limitations"*;[9] and *"taking another step across the threshold of the heavens"* (italics added)[10]—all of which orient us through an up-down vertical pattern and a merger of space and earth. Centered around a contradiction between the discovery of the moon and the discovery of the earth, these images first create the illusion of individuals reaching upward and then mirror in that illusion a projected thrust downward.

Consider, for instance, a metaphor like *reaching with precision for the moon* and *falling into raucous discord on earth*. It is powerful in exposing the contradiction between space discovery and earth activities, and in motivating one to adopt both a personal and public philosophy of what is "enough." Quite literally, the metaphor argues that our *reaching* or stretching beyond ourselves for space—something that once was extemely important—now contrasts drastically with our life on earth. The image that is activated is that while we have demonstrated excellence in space, we have neglected the concerns of earth.

Beyond mere literal interpretation, the power of the metaphor to motivate one to act against our current attitudes toward the space program takes its shape from the experiences of physical and historical oppression that it activates. Physically, the metaphor individuates the excitement of reaching up, striving, going beyond, and being exact, and the frustration with what lies below—failing. Who, for instance, has not experienced the phenomenon of reaching for something that lay just out of reach, only to stumble to the ground having seized the prize; who has not put a great deal of time and energy into achieving a goal, only to discover that the end did not justify the means? In this metaphor, the upward motion of the space program serves to heighten a move downward; by dialectic implication, the metaphor entertains the possibility of a situation in which the space program is not burdensome or akin to domestic failure.

The physical push upward toward excellence is not the only aspect of the metaphor that angles the individual downward; the downward thrust is complemented as well by the emotions extracted from our understanding of the times. It calls our attention, in other words, to the dissension: to the din of angry voices, the protests, and the assassinations happening on earth. As the precision of the moon landings pushes against the chaotic state of earth, the metaphor remakes us into people who are fed up with the protests, the demonstrators, the riots, the disorder, and the chaos. We are transformed, in other words, into individuals who will no longer tolerate the current state of affairs—especially given that we can reach for the moon with such exactness. The metaphor motivates the American people to enact a posture of "enough" and to work toward a new inter-pretation of the space program.

Throwing wide the horizons of space we discovered new horizons of earth reveals a complementary up-down pattern as well as a side-to-side movement. Having gone to the moon, we are now confronted by the image of a person who stands at a door, hesitates but a moment, and then gives a tug and opens it wide. It asks us to compare our approach to space with our approach to earth, and to realize that they are the same, and yet different. It is designed to make us think of the bold ways in which we as Americans stood at the gates of the new frontier, paused but a moment, and then blasted off into space.

Such an image transforms our understanding of space. Outer space is remade into a vantage point from which we now view the earth: Space becomes not the end goal but the lens by which we can now consider other things. Again, a common experience is invoked: Who has not had the experience of climbing to the top of a hill and then turning around and surveying the trek upward? Nixon works to establish a new perspective for the space program, quite literally, by asking us to take a new look at our past treks. These images invite us to look, think, see, compare, and realize.

The heavens have become a part of man's world[11] typifies the movement contained in the juxtaposition of moon exploration with concern for the earth, and goes farther than the previous two examples by making the connection explicit. Here, the upward movement to the moon actually becomes a part of the downward thrust to the earth; what is up is down. We are not stretched as in the first example; there is no sense of pressure or failure. Rather, there is a sense of unity, a sense in which the entire universe is brought into the purview of humanity.

These images make us look up and then down; they make us think about where we have come and where we might be going; they focus attention on the discovery of the moon and, in the process, they ask us to discover the earth. The calmness and perfection contained in reaching for the moon contrasts with the violence and disorder on earth, and a gaping hole between the two is created. As Nixon brings the moon into the realm of earth, and vice versa, the gulf between them begins to disappear. Metaphorically, in other words, Nixon both creates and then offers a solution to the gulf separating the earth and the moon. Such images establish Nixon as the one with the vision, the one with the master plan.

Wonderment Lost and Found

In contrast to the first cluster of images which exploits the up–down pattern to create an understanding of a "successful moon experience" and a troubled earth in need of a new perspective, the second cluster emphasizes the necessity of continued space exploration. What initially seems a contradiction (in terms of the first cluster) soon becomes the basis for a whole new approach to space exploration to be taken by the United States. These images play about the edges of the recent moon landings and work to renew energy and excitement in the area of space exploration.

Initially, Nixon invoked what appears to be the Columbus Principle. Following the successful launch of *Apollo 14*, Nixon stated:

In a way we are like the people who must have stood on the dock at Palos, Spain, and watched Columbus's ships disappear, believing they were watching the end of a great event, when they were watching the beginning. But where they watched the world being opened and did not know it, we are watching the heavens being opened and we do know it. It was the end of a great event when it was the beginning—we know ours to be a great event.[12]

This, however, is not the experience of discovery for discovery's sake. Rather, here we are united with, and yet separated from, our past. We are like our ancestors in that we watch events of exploration take place, and yet history has given us a new perspective. We can view the past with hindsight. We know, unlike the people who watched Columbus sail away, that the earth was not flat, and more significantly, we know that Columbus actually did something fantastic in discovering a new world. It is our knowledge, the passage suggests, that differentiates us from those who came before us.

Simultaneously, the intermingling of beginnings and endings is appealing precisely because we have all had some sort of experience with something we thought was over—only to discover that it was actually what led to something else. We have a sense here of the passage of time, of a process where beginnings give way to endings, which in turn give way to new beginnings. Moreover, again, these images invite us to adopt a new perspective, the perspective of contemplative knowledge. To become a part all we need do is look and think.

That this yearning for exploration is contained in our makeup is never questioned by Nixon but rather is invoked as proof that we must continue to discover. Every lunar liftoff *"reflects our restless quest for beginnings"*;[13] *"reenacts another, deeper ritual"*;[14] exposes the *"primal need in man's blood to know from where we've come"*;[15] *"proves man's invincible will to master the moment of his destiny"*;[16] and *"brings tribute to man's unquenchable thirst for understanding"* (italics added).[17] Such phrases are filled with emotionalism, especially in a president known for his factual in information. However, while these images tap into unique human experiences—the search for our roots, the quest to figure out exactly who we are, the desire to get to the essence and center of life—they do not quite motivate to action. The images, in other words, do not contain kernels of action but rather kernels of knowledge; they expose wonderment.

The sense of wonderment is augmented by the force of history. Nixon stated:

We had little idea what *lay before* us, but there was new knowledge to be *gained* and there was a *heritage of meeting historical challenge*—the challenge of greatness—*to be sustained*. We are *taking another long step* in man's *ancient search* for his own beginnings, *pressing beyond* knowledge of the means of human existence to find, perhaps, the meaning of human existence. . . . the *making* of space history will continue, and this Nation *means to play* a major role in its making. (italics added)[18]

Again, the images are descriptive rather than posed toward action. Again they tell us that a precedent has already been established and that our posture ought to be one of staying the course. We need not, then, be any more creative or ingenious than we were in the past; we need merely to sustain our previous goal.

Within this cluster of images there unfolds a drama whereby the American people become "tenders" of space. In invoking an elevated sense of knowledge, the essence of human nature, and historical precedent, Nixon establishes a rationale for a continued space effort. While this cluster of images, like the previous cluster, asks us to stop and look, it also asks us to continue on. The question then becomes how we can continue on if we must also stop and look; how, in other words, we can make a beginning out of an ending. It is here, then, that a third cluster of metaphors becomes operational, a cluster capable of completing the transformation from wonderment to pragmatics.

The Extraordinary Becomes Routine

Perhaps the most unique and inviting characteristic of metaphor is the way in which it brings together and resolves contradictory experiences. No other process, in fact, is expressly designed for such a task. Thus, in Nixon's rhetoric, the idea of stopping to look and think about the commonalities of the moon and earth not only meets the concept of continued exploration, but easily interacts with and comfortably lives side by side with it. This is possible because a third cluster of metaphors creates an image of the U.S. space program as ordinary and routine. In bringing the space program to earth, Nixon is able to make it a continuous part of our everyday experiences. We are asked, then, to explore, but our exploration must be tempered with an interest in earth; in other words, we must be able to connect our exploration to the earth. This cluster is activated by the language of business: Nixon asks that we "think of the space program not only as an adventure of today, but as an investment in tomorrow."[19] Space activities become, then:

A *part* of our lives for the *rest of time;* we must think of them as *part of a continuing process*—one which will go on *day in and day out, year in and year out*—not as a *series of separate leaps*, each requiring a *massive concentration of energy* and will and accomplished on a *crash timetable*. What we do in space from here on in must become a *normal and regular part* of our national life and must therefore be *planned in conjunction* with all of the other undertakings which are also important. They must take their place within a *rigorous system* of national priorities. (italics added)[20]

Clearly, this paragraph works to make the act of space exploration commonplace; indeed, it takes something that is extraordinary—going to the moon—and argues that it is a true part of
life. It is an easy step to move from the notion that discovery is a
part of the human experience, and that discovery is a continuous process, to a desire to make the space program compatible.
This image is enhanced with the notion of day in–day out, year
in–year out. Our space program ought to be not just daily, but
almost mundane.

It is into this milieu that Nixon introduces the concept of the
space shuttle, and it is into this milieu that the space shuttle
concept becomes readily acceptable. The shuttle, Nixon
explains, is

a new type of space transportation system designed to help *transform*
the *space frontier* of the 1970s into *familiar territory, easily accessible for
human endeavor* in the 1980s and 90s. It will *revolutionize* transportation
into near space by *routinizing* it. It will take the *astronomical* costs out of
astronautics. In short, it will go a long way toward delivering the rich
benefits of practical space utilization and the valuable spinoffs from
space efforts into the daily lives of Americans and all people. (italics
added)[21]

The passage is appealing in part because of our experiences with
the concepts of the new frontier and the space frontier, and our
understanding of familiar territory. Such a passage calls
attention not only to the pioneers who crossed the plains but to
those who did the same in space. It plays on our understanding
that experience itself creates knowledge, and that knowledge in
turn leads to familiarity. We know what space is like, the images
continue to suggest, and thus need to focus not on exploration
per se, but on getting on with the process of living. What was
special is now ordinary.

The vision of the United States and its space program that
Nixon's metaphors create is a complete one. It takes us from the
realization that the discovery of the moon cannot occur without
a simultaneous discovery of the earth, it brings us face to face
with the understanding that our quest for understanding is a
mainstay of the American character, and it forces us to accept
that we have moved beyond the pioneering stage and must now
work on improving our efforts.

Nixon's vision of the United States is not especially powerful or compelling. The images are common and easy to visualize, and yet they bring about no real action. The images make sense, and yet they do not call for much activity. We are not asked to participate in the space program per se; rather, we are asked to contemplate it. We are no longer the spectators filling the stadium and cheering the program on, but have become the strategists who think and plan, invest and maintain. Thus, while Nixon's decision to move to a reusable space shuttle was a most economical choice—indeed, the best choice given the times; and while Nixon's metaphors created a sound backdrop against which the shuttle made sense, that decision and those metaphors essentially killed public interest in the program. In taking away our pioneering posture and in making our need to explore part of our everyday characteristics, Nixon removed the awe surrounding the space program. Whereas a decade earlier, the program had been elevated to a special position in life, now it was no different than education, housing, or any other governmental concern. While the movement from pioneer to nonpioneer did indeed dampen interest in the space program, it alone was not responsible. The entire complex of Nixon's metaphors must be considered. Had Nixon been able to fashion a more active United States and a more active American citizen, he might have been able to rekindle the excitement of an earlier decade. As a pragmatic man interested in letting the facts speak for themselves, however, he could only create an image of the contemplative person who did little more than think. He left to his predecessors the task of "activating" the public to a pro-space posture.

FORD CONTRIBUTES TO A BETTER TOMORROW

Of all the presidents involved in the U.S. program of space exploration, Gerald Ford contributed the least. Ford's situation was, however, unique. He had assumed the vice presidential position shortly after Spiro Agnew was forced to resign in October 1973. Less than a year later, on the eve of Nixon's resignation (which was induced by the Watergate scandal), he assumed the presidency. Under normal circumstances, Ford would have brought the vice presidential experiences as head of the President's Space Council to bear. Time, however, did not afford him the luxury of such experience, and he was forced to scramble to come to terms with the history of the space program.

As it turned out, Ford spent much of his tenure as president trying to move the nation beyond the crisis of Watergate. His pardon of Nixon, while admittedly ill-conceived and ill-timed, was indicative of his desire to get the country moving again, and so too was his rhetoric of space exploration.[22] Indeed, using the experiences of the two space adventures which occurred while he was in office, *Skylab* and the Soviet-U.S. space linkup, Ford fashioned the space program as a springboard for a better future.

Looking Skyward

A quick look through Ford's rhetoric of space reveals a myriad of images that ask us to *look upward* and *extend our vision*. Upon receiving a crystal that was grown aboard the space station *Skylab*, for instance, Ford stated:

Most of us become so involved in trying to *find* solutions to the serious problems that we *face* today that we sometimes *lose sight* of the developments that *hold promise* for a better tomorrow. This [crystal] is a *reminder* that we should *raise our sights* to the *broadening horizons* available to us through our *national investments* in science and technology. (italics added)[23]

The visionary images again come to the fore in Ford's statements at the dedication of the bicentennial exposition of science and technology at the Kennedy Space Center in Florida. "This exposition," he stated, "will *show* Americans that our *horizons* are still *unlimited,* and so is our *capacity to reach* for them into our third century."[24] Finally, upon presenting the Goddard Memorial Trophy to the *Skylab* astronauts, Ford made his visionary appeal once again.

I am a *complete believer* in the accomplishments, the mission of a good, fine, *forward-looking, visionary* space program for America. It is basically

a *reward* for the *faith* that the American people have had in what we
have to do *in looking skyward, down the road,* for a bigger and better world
in which we can all live. (italics added)[25]

Centered around a contradiction between seeing and not
seeing, between reaching and not reaching, and between limiting
and not limiting, these images create the illusion of individuals
struggling for a new vision. Consider the image of the *Skylab*
crystal as a *reminder* that we should *raise our sights.* Like some of
Nixon's images, this image powerfully exposes the contradiction between space discovery and earthly activities. However, rather than motivating us to adopt a philosophy of
"enough," it actually motivates us to adopt an attitude of
"more." Such an image argues that we have "forgotten" what
exploits in space can produce, and bids us take a new look.

This image also goes beyond literal interpretation and draws
its support from the experiences of physical and social ineptness
that it activates. Physically, the metaphor invokes the activity of
looking for a particular item and the frustration of not being able
to find it. Who, for instance, has not had the experience of
searching for a lost item only to find it after the search was over;
who has not had the opportunity to say, "If it was a snake, it
would have bitten me"? Within this image we are cast into a
nation of seekers and Ford becomes the one with the answers.
Thus, what is *overlooked* can be *found*; what is *invisible* can become
visible. The image motivates us to reconsider the space program;
indeed, it argues that the answers to our earthly dilemmas lie in
the stars.

Seeing Is Not Believing

Ford's visionary images were probably appropriate for the
time. Historian Jules Witcover argued that "there was some
thing very refreshing about this natural and open man, after five
years of the self-conscious, awkward, posturing Nixon," and
that with his presidency, "a sense of relief swept over the deep
gloom that had shrouded the federal city and the nation through
the last dark year of the Nixon reign."[26] A visionary, however,
must have something to show, and Ford did not have enough.
What he had us *raising our sights* for and *looking at* were not items
thought to bring a better tomorrow.

A crystal, for instance, did not appear to have much significance. Beyond the crystal, Ford could not come up with meaty enough examples of payoffs and rewards. He stated, for instance:

When we *look* at what we can *do* with science, whether it is in climate or energy, in food, in health, or a wide variety of other areas, we should be *emphasizing very dramatically* to the people who will come and see it, *the prospects for a better life* in 1976 and for the next 100 years thereafter. (italics added)[27]

However, the only concrete example given was of the crystal grown aboard *Skylab*, hardly a fitting example for the majority of people.

In his 1977 study of Ford's War on Inflation campaign, Hermann Stelzner argued that the campaign's failure lay "not in Ford's lack of personal commitment to it, but in his inability to 'work it.' . . . Ford could not portray the severity of the crisis and did not propose short-term, precise, realistic incentives for engaging the enemy."[28] In other words, by not fully understanding the nature of the systems of associations called into play by the war metaphor, Ford's war on inflation could not sustain itself, and thus gave way to more viable and complete depictions of the economy.

In a similar vein, Ford was also unable to exploit the image of looking to space for a better tomorrow. Perhaps with more time or under different circumstances he could have been successful. In the short term, however, Ford probably did more to damage the space program than to help it. Because he could not come up with significant images of how space was contributing to a better tomorrow, our "raised sights" were not appeased. Indeed, it may very well have been Ford's less than palatable images that enabled Jimmy Carter to declare that space would now be put into service for public use.

CARTER TAKES A PRUDENT STAND

When Carter politicked for the presidency, he did so as an outsider. He wanted the American people to know that he was not like the Washington insiders; that he had a fresh way of looking at political and social events and that he was untainted by big money or big interest. True to his word, Carter went out of his way to "keep in touch with the American people."[29] He worked in his shirtsleeves, walked instead of driving, visited people in their offices, held relaxed televised fireside chats, sent his daughter to public school, and lobbied for a space program that could deliver a public dividend. The wonderment of space exploration emphasized by earlier presidents dropped out of Carter's vision altogether, and as a result, the program of space exploration merged into our program of earth exploration.

Space at an Affordable Price

Like Nixon, Carter focused his attention on earthbound issues. However, whereas Nixon projected us as thinkers pondering the connection between the wonders of space exploration and the use of space exploits, Carter turned us into penny-pinching accountants and cost-managers, with one eye on space expenditures and the other on space benefits.

The space shuttle provided the impetus for change. Carter admitted that he liked the shuttle precisely because of its money-saving potential. Early on in his presidency, he presaged a theme that would stay with his program of space exploration for the duration. "I'm interested in the shuttle program," he said. "It's going to be a much *cheaper means* by which we can perform our very valuable flights in space and still return the *costly* vehicle back to Earth (italics added)."[30] Here, two contradictory images are juxtaposed. On the one hand we are asked to look at the shuttle as if it were a *bargain*. On the other, we are asked to remember that it is *expensive*. The image seems to turn on the ambiguity provided in the notion of *valuable flights*. We are asked to question the extent to which this *expensive/bargain* space flight is of value to us. The image has us looking both ways, side to side, questioning.

Additional images that emerge out of our understanding of money management continue to play a key role for Carter in shaping our understanding of the space shuttle and the space program. At issue, Carter states, is how to best *"capitalize on prior investments,''*[31] how to *''make our explorations more efficient as far as the dollars spent compared to the results obtained,''*[32] and how *''to change dramatic, very costly initiatives into a sound, progressive, and innovative program''*[33] (italics added).

What is interesting about these metaphors is that they do not tap into the most common of American experiences. As much as Carter wanted to keep in touch with the American people, his images appealed to a much smaller group. The language of business that backs Carter's thoughts invokes the image of the money manager, the accountant, the financial advisor, or the CEO rather than the household budgeter, the person who "pays the bills," or even the one who balances the checkbook. While we may wonder if "we've made the right investment," or if "we've done the right thing," only a handful of us will ask if we've *capitalized on prior investments*. The average person, in other words, is overlooked in favor of the financial accountant assessing the state of investments in search of "the bottom line." As Carter told a gathering of scientists, "In the coming era we will reap a good return on what we have invested in space."[34]

Adventure Becomes Routine

As one set of Carter's images worked to turn the American people into fiscal mangers, a second worked to alter our thinking about the nature of space exploits. In particular, we were asked to think of space exploits as routine rather than special events.

Consider some of Carter's statements. During a question-and-answer session in Portsmouth, New Hampshire, Carter explained that the most exciting thing about this next great era in space was that the use of space would become routine rather than a great adventure every time a craft was launched.[35] To the Communications Workers of America, he stated that "we're shifting toward a more routine way to deal with space and the space shuttle. We now have a way at a reasonable price to have routine trips into space and back."[36] Moreover, during a "call-out" program on National Public Radio, Carter noted, "We've derived tremendous personal benefits from the experiment and innovations that went into earlier space flights . . . but now we're going into a more routine space use."[37]

The motivating force behind these statements lies in the way in which the images continuously supplant the energy and excitement of previous space exploits in favor of routinization. As *adventure* merges with *costly* and *personal benefits*, *routine* comes to be associated with *efficient* and *public benefits*. Working within this set of contradictory experiences, we come to the realization that what is adventuresome can be routine; what is costly can be efficient, and what is personal can also be public. What is important here is that Carter does not ask us to give up the idea of adventure, but rather to realize that routinization is predicated on adventure. First comes adventure, and then routine. Speaking to editors and news directors, Carter made his position clear:

So we're not going to minimize or decrease our commitment to space; the spectacular efforts to send men to the moon have been a precursor to the more practical and consistent and effective use of our space technology. . . . [I]t's not a matter of playing down the importance of space, it's a matter of using what we've learned in the most effective way.[38]

Becoming Earthbound

Cast into a drama in which we question the value of costly space flights, learn that adventure has a place in routinization, and work to become more fiscally responsible, our activities are turned away from space and centered on earth.

The image of an earthbound people emerges during some remarks Carter gave at the Congressional Space Medal of Honor awards ceremonies. "The first great era of the space age is over, the second is about to begin," he stated. "During Apollo we were pilgrims in space, ranging far from home in search of knowledge. Now we will become shepherds tending our technological flocks, but like the shepherds of old, we will keep our eyes fixed on the heavens."[39] The transformation from heaven to earth is vividly accomplished as Carter asserts a new identity for us. No longer will we be those who have embarked on a lofty adventure; now we will stay behind and "mind the store." Carter does leave open the possibility of freeing the bonds to Earth, but we are made aware that it will not be soon. Rather than wonderment, these notions create a sense of longing.

Carter's images went a long way in forging an understanding of an accountable, routine, earthbound space program. In erring on the side of financial accountability, however, Carter destroyed the "glory of exploration." As indicated throughout all of his metaphors of cost cutting, routinization, and watchful shepherding, wonderment is relegated to a past era (as well as an era that may come about in the future), and earthly priorities and longing are the order of the day. Longing, however, is not the same as wonderment. It creates frustration rather than excitement and dissatisfaction instead of awe.

Carter made it clear during his tenure as president that it was "neither feasible nor necessary at this time to commit the United States to a high-challenge space engineering initiative."[40] He made it clear that we needed to keep our nose to the grindstone and get the job done. Without a sense of wonderment, however, Carter's program of space exploration became little more than a grind. Judging by the constant schedule mishaps and design delays that postponed the development of the first shuttle, it would seem that those at NASA also thought the program to be little more than a job. Changing the direction that Carter had set would not be an easy task, for it required a president with a keen sense of vision. Luckily, as if specifically designed to fit that bill, Ronald Reagan succeeded to the presidency.

NOTES

1. Howard Benedict, "Landing End of Long Road," *Duluth News Tribune*, 16 July 1989, IE.

2. "Text of Address by Nixon in San Francisco Assessing Challenge of Soviet Satellite," *New York Times* 16 Oct. 1957, TK.

3. See Richard W. Fox and T. Jackson Lears, eds., *The Culture of Consumption* (New York: Pantheon, 1983), 205.

4. *National Space Program: Report of the Select House Committee on Astronautics and Space Exploration* (Washington, D.C.: U.S. Government Printing Office, 1958), 3.

5. Richard Nixon, "Inaugural Address," 20 Jan. 1969, *Public Papers of*

the Presidents of the United States, Richard M. Nixon, 1969 (Washington, D.C.: U.S. Government Printing Office, 1971), 2. (Hereafter abbreviated *PPP, RMN, year.*)

6. Nixon, "Inaugural Address," *PPP, RMN, 1969,* 1.

7. Nixon, "Inaugural Address," *PPP, RMN, 1969,* 4.

8. Ibid.

9. Richard Nixon, "Address at the Air Force Academy Commencement Exercises in Colorado Springs, Colorado," 4 June 1969, *PPP, RMN, 1969,* 432-37.

10. Richard Nixon, "Statement Following the Successful Launch of Apollo 15," 26 July, 1971, *PPP, RMN, 1971* (Washington, D.C.: U.S. Government Printing Office, 1972), 826.

11. Richard Nixon, "Telephone Conversation with the Apollo 11 Astronauts on the Moon," 20 July 1969, *PPP, RMN, 1969,* 530.

12. Richard Nixon, "Statement Following the Successful Launch of Apollo 14," 31 Jan. 1971, *PPP, RMN, 1971,* 96-97.

13. Nixon, "Launch of Apollo 15," *PPP, RMN, 1971,* 826.

14. Ibid.

15. Ibid.

16. Richard Nixon, "Statement Following the Splashdown of Apollo 15," 7 Aug. 1971, *PPP, RMN, 1971,* 885.

17. Ibid.

18. Richard Nixon, "Statement about the Space Program," 19 December 1972, *PPP, RMN, 1972* (Washington, D.C.: U.S. Government Printing Office, 1974), 1157.

19. Richard Nixon, "Statement about the Future of the United States Space Program," 7 Mar. 1970, *PPP, RMN, 1970* (Washington, D.C.: Government Printing Office, 1971), 250-53.

20. Ibid.

21. Richard Nixon, "Statement Announcing Decision to Proceed with Development of the Space Shuttle," 5 Jan. 1972, *PPP, RMN, 1972,* 20-21.

22. Jules Witcover, *Marathon: The Pursuit of the Presidency 1972-1976* (New York: Viking, 1977), 35-45.

23. Gerald R. Ford, "Statement on Receiving a Crystal Grown Aboard the Skylab Space Station," 4 Nov. 1974, *Public Papers of the Presidents of the United States, Gerald R. Ford, 1974* (Washington, D.C.: U.S. Government Printing Office, 1975), 577. (Hereafter abbreviated *PPP, GRF, year.*)

24. Gerald Ford, "Telephone Remarks on the Dedication of the Bicentennial Exposition on Science and Technology at the Kennedy Space Center in Florida," 14 June 1976, *PPP, GRF, 1976-77,* vol. II (Washington, D.C.: U.S. Government Printing Office, 1979), 1873.

25. Gerald Ford, "Remarks upon Presenting the Goddard Memorial Trophy to the Skylab Astronauts," 11 Apr. 1975, *PPP, GRF, 1975*, vol I (Washington, D.C.: U.S. Government Printing Office, 1977), 474.

26. Witcover, *Marathon*, 14.

27. Gerald Ford, "Remarks at a Meeting on the Bicentennial Exposition on Science and Technology," 9 Feb. 1976, *PPP, GRF, 1976-77*, vol. I (Washington, D.C.: U.S. Government Printing Office, 1979), 239.

28. Hermann G. Stelzner, "Ford's War on Inflation: A Metaphor that Did Not Cross," *Communication Monographs* 44 (1977): 285.

29. Witcover, *Marathon*, 656.

30. James E. Carter, "Remarks during a Telephone Call-In Program on the CBS Radio Network," 5 Mar. 1977, *Public Papers of the Presidents of the United States, James E. Carter, 1977*, vol. I (Washington, D.C.: U.S. Government Printing Office, 1977), 48. (Hereafter abbreviated *PPP, JEC, year*.)

31. James E. Carter, "Announcement of Administration Review of U.S. Space Activities," 20 June 1978, *PPP, JEC, 1978*, vol. II (Washington, D.C.: U.S. Government Printing Office, 1979), 1135.

32. James E. Carter, "Q & A Session at a Town Hall Meeting in Berlin, Federal Republic of Germany," 15 July 1978, *PPP, JEC, 1978*, II: 1303.

33. James E. Carter, "Remarks and a Q & A Session with Editors and News Directors," 13 Oct. 1978, *PPP, JEC, 1978*, II: 1776-77.

34. James E. Carter, "Remarks at the National Academy of Sciences Annual Meeting," 23 April 1979, *PPP, JEC, 1979*, vol. I (Washington, D.C.: U.S. Government Printing Office, 1980), 681.

35. James E. Carter, "Remarks and a Q & A Session at a Town Meeting in Portsmouth, New Hampshire," 25 April 1979, *PPP, JEC, 1979*, I: 712.

36. James E. Carter, "Remarks and a Q & A Session at the Annual Convention of the Communications Workers of America," 16 July 1979, *PPP, JEC, 1979*, vol. II (Washington, D.C.: U.S. Government Printing Office, 1980), 1250-51.

37. James E. Carter, "Remarks during a Telephone Call-Out Program on National Public Radio," 13 Oct. 1979, *PPP, JEC, 1979*, II: 1912.

38. James E. Carter, "Remarks and a Q & A Session with Editors and News Directors," 13 Oct. 1978, *PPP, JEC, 1978*, II: 1777.

39. James E. Carter, "Remarks at the Congressional Space Medal of Honor Awards Ceremony," 1 Oct. 1978, *PPP, JEC, 1978*, II: 1687.

40. Howard E. McCurdy, *The Space Station Decision* (Baltimore: Johns Hopkins University Press, 1990), 58.

Chapter Four

Starting a Nation Dreaming Again

When Ronald Reagan was elected president, NASA officials breathed a sigh of relief. For eleven years, the period of time that had elapsed since the first astronaut stepped onto the moon and support for the space program began to diminish, NASA had been forced to engage in incremental politics. With dismay, they watched as the final three Apollo missions were scrubbed; as the three-tiered project of space station, space shuttle, and moon base became the shuttle; and as interest in a mission to Mars was relegated to the back burner.[1] Reagan, however, appeared to be a true believer in space. "Like President Kennedy before him," Howard McCurdy stated, "Reagan seemed genuinely entranced by the space program. NASA officials could only hope that he might make an Apollo-type decision as President Kennedy had done two decades earlier."[2]

Ironically, in terms of concrete decisions and actual deeds, Reagan did not actually do anything for the space program. He did come close to making an Apollo-type decision by calling for a manned space station, and he did authorize NASA to build a shuttle orbiter to replace the one destroyed in the *Challenger* explosion. He also got us thinking about "space shields," but beyond that, no tangible results were amassed. Rather, what Reagan did for the space program was to revitalize it. With his metaphors, Reagan created a palatable vision of a U.S. space program "standing tall" and simultaneously brought renewed energy and a new vitality to the program. Rhetorically, at least, the program prospered under Reagan.

This chapter explores how Reagan whetted our appetites for space exploration once again. Specifically, it suggests that the key to Reagan's transformation of space resides in the way in which he used the notion of *the new frontier*. Nearly three decades earlier, Frank Gibney and George Feldman had argued that the space program would prosper only if it were tied to a frontier image. "This country has always prospered because it had a frontier to chew on," they suggested. "The Space Discovery represents the only possible frontier of any magnitude at hand today, yet we have rejected its potential out of hand."[3] Now we finally had a president in place who was willing to argue exclusively for the importance of this concept. Indeed, not only did Reagan argue for this *new frontier* perspective on space, he did so through two vital areas of national life: commercialization and militarization. Focusing on Reagan's space rhetoric up until the explosion of the space shuttle *Challenger*, this chapter explores his revitalizing perspective.

COMMERCIALIZING SPACE

Reagan, it would seem, was lucky. He always seemed to be at the right place at the right time, and he was able to use that timing to his advantage. On the day he was sworn in as president, for instance, the Iran hostage situation, which had dogged Carter's presidency for nearly two years, resolved itself. Similarly, Reagan's first days in office coincided perfectly with the testing of the first shuttle prototype and the maiden flight of the first operational shuttle. Each successive shuttle flight provided Reagan with the opportunity to hone his message that it was "time to develop the next frontier—space."[4] In particular, his images developed this understanding of space by depicting a nation of individuals who are "pushing back boundaries" so that "the desert will bloom."[5]

Pushing Back Boundaries

In *Verbal Style and the Presidency*, Roderick Hart argued that Reagan's images are active images; they depict us as working when in fact we may not be doing anything at all.[6] That seems to be the case with Reagan's space rhetoric; within his images, we are cast as "movers and shakers" who are single-handedly pushing back the new frontier, single-handedly clearing the land for the new civilization to follow.

A glance through Reagan's rhetoric reveals metaphorical images such as: *"part of a greatness pushing wider the boundaries";*[7] *"never a time when we can stop moving forward";*[8] *"pushing back frontiers and opening new doors to discovery, opportunity, and progress;"*[9] *"blazing the trail to an exciting new frontier;"*[10] and *"discovering new horizons"*[11] (italics added). Centered around a contradiction between *moving* and *standing still*, these images invite us to discover a new world. Indeed, they suggest that we are already discovering that world and only have to continue.

Consider, for instance, *pushing back frontiers and opening new doors to discovery, opportunity, and progress.* The image is powerful in the way in which it casts us into a situation where we are not only actively moving forward but also reaping the benefits. Literally, the metaphor argues that by continuing forward and going beyond whatever obstacles might be in our way, new discoveries will be ours. It puts us into a situation in which by pushing, we attain new things.

Beyond this literal interpretation, the power of the metaphor to motivate us into thinking new thoughts about the space pro-gram emerges from the experiences of physical and historical excitement that it activates. Physically, the metaphor individu-ates the excitement of an individual moving forward, arms extended out in front and head bent slightly forward, pushing on. Most of us have experienced the sensation of pushing through a thicket of bushes to get to the other side, or of pushing through a wind storm to reach a destiny. *Pushing,* by its nature, does not allow for *standing still.* We may stand, in other words, in front of a thicket of bushes, but standing will not grant us passage. Similarly, we may go out into a wind storm, but if we do not push forward we will not make any headway. This metaphor, then, motivates us toward a renewed look at the space program by entertaining the possibility of a situation in which discoveries are not occurring because there is no forward motion.

The image of *pushing back frontiers* motivates as well from the way in which it ignites historical and social experiences of a past and present time. The very fact that Reagan refers to space as a *frontier* takes us back to an earlier time when the United States was a young country, undiscovered by our ancestors. The image calls attention to the kinds of discoveries that were made when Davy Crocket, Daniel Boone, and Meriwether Lewis and George Clark trudged across the land. Out of a wilderness frontier, these explorers created a modern civilization. It implies that if the notion of the frontier worked for them, then by dialectical implication, it certainly could work for us now.

In taking us back to the past, this image simultaneously bids us to look to the present and consider the frontier possibilities now available. The excitement of adventure on which this image of the frontier plays also asks us to compare the kind of space program we have had with the kind we could have. In particular, this image asks us to think about the stark vision of space that Carter laid out, about the difference between *shepherding* and *making a pilgrimage*. Here Reagan puts some character back into the starkness of Carter's space policies.

Finally, the motivating power of the images of *pushing back the frontier* comes from the way in which they assert an identity for all Americans. Consider this passage from Reagan's remarks at a National Space Club Luncheon:

The *challenge* of *pushing back frontiers* is *part* of our *national character*. As we face the vast expanses of space, let us *recapture those stirrings* in our soul *that make us Americans*. Space, like freedom, is a limitless, never ending *frontier* on which *our citizens can prove* they are indeed *Americans*. (italics added)[12]

Such ideas transform the new frontier—space—into a proving ground. They individuate the emotionalism of pitting ourselves against nature, demonstrating what we're really made of, and showing we're strong. What emerges, as well, is a sense of pride in being called an American. The identity thus forged is clear: Americans are a unique breed, with character and chutzpa. Accepting Reagan's vision of space then becomes a way of claiming this kind of identity. As Reagan stated at a ceremony commemorating the Bicentennial Year of Air and Space Flight, "We Americans have always been at our best when we've faced challenge—exploring and taming new frontiers, testing our talents and abilities, and yes, moving on. We're a nation that lionizes pathfinders."[13]

Failing to explore, tame, or test our talents and abilities is regarded within Reagan's vision as a failure of character. Consider his rhetoric. "Today we stand on the edge of a world in which opportunities are limited only by our own imagination,"[14] Reagan states. "Nothing binds our abilities except our expectations, and given that, the farthest star is within our reach,"[15] he contends. In other words, the vision and glory of proving ourselves in space is there for the taking. The only obstacle is our inability to imagine and dream the impossible. We are already moving forward, already on the verge of experiencing the excitement and character building of the new frontier. All we have to do now is overcome our own limits.

The opening up of this new frontier is connected, then, to the enhancement of our national character. At the same time, it is linked to the enhancement of our national position. As we take the "space challenge" and prove that we are good and worthy Americans, we simultaneously demonstrate our interest in furthering the interests of the American nation.

Making the Desert Bloom

A passage from a speech delivered by Reagan at the National Space Club Luncheon in March 1985 brings these dual contextualizations—individual American character and national American character—together:

individual freedom and the *profit motive* were the *engines of progress* which *transformed* an American *wilderness* into an *economic dynamo* that provided the American people with a *standard* of living that is still the *envy of the world*. . . . We must make sure the same *incentives* that worked so well in *developing* America's *first frontier* are brought into play in *taming the frontier of space*. (italics added)[16]

Literally, this passage argues that our individual character and concern with commercialization are the elements capable of turning outer space into a spectacular and enviable phenomenon. The individual metaphors, *engines of progress, economic dynamo, envy of the world,* and *taming the frontier* are quintessentially Reagan. Although they are overused figures of speech, they are nevertheless powerful because they tap into the most basic of our common experiences. As a result, they forge a very dramatic and compelling vision. The United States is not just dynamic in the area of commerce, it is a *dynamo.* Progress does not just happen, it is backed by the force of an *engine.* The frontier is not just settled, it is *tamed.* Clearly such images activate individual action in the service of character and national interests.

A second passage also demonstrates the motivating character of the commercialization aspect of the frontier image. In a radio address to the nation on commercial space initiatives, Reagan stated: "We are now *ready* to *make the desert bloom.* We have *cultivated* space for the past 25 years and now is the *harvest time.* Now is the time to *reap the practical fruits of* all that *daring"*(italics added).[17] Cast within the language of growth, these images again ask us to think differently about the development of space.

Consider the metaphoric quality of *making the desert bloom.* The image is most appropriate in sharpening our understanding about the potential success of commercial exploits in space. The oxymoronic quality of this image invokes a picture of a not-too-long-ago lunar landing and the way in which our presence on the moon brought the desolation of the lunar dust to life. Visions of Neil Armstrong and Buzz Aldrin bouncing about on the moon, taking pictures, and scooping up rocks merge with images of Alan Shepard and Jim Lovell hitting golf balls and riding moon carts. *Making the desert bloom* makes the moon come alive with activity and asserts that such activity can happen again.

At the same time, this image puts us in a situation where we can, literally, make some assessments about the ways in which we have made the deserts in Arizona, New Mexico, and southern California come to life. The sense of human endeavor that is a part of *cultivate* and *harvest time* also adds to the idea that space can be enhanced and a profit can be amassed. Here is a vision in which people are working to make things happen.

The New World Again

The combined images of the American character working to enhance the American nation result in what can only be considered a reindividuation of the New World. One final passage from Reagan's rhetoric of "commercial space" underscores and enhances the result of this merger. At the end of his remarks at the Goddard Space Center, Reagan stated: "We must always be the New World—the world of discovery, that reveres the great truths of its past and looks forward with unending faith to the promise of the future. America will remain future's child, the golden hope for all mankind."[18]

Here is a passage filled with the sort of lofty vision that Carter was never able to amass for the space program. Here is America "standing tall" with a renewed sense of purpose and vitality. The passage nurtures a sense of pride that comes from being an American, while at the same time cultivating an understanding of stature that comes from the American nation. In typical Reagan fashion, the thoughts put forward conjure up images of a youthful vibrant America of a time gone by, and by contrast suggest that this posture is ours for the taking. Indeed, we are permanently recast into that youthful, vibrant nation via the image of *future's child* and the *golden hope*.

Reagan's metaphorical images promoted a renewed vitality in our program of outer space exploration. He brought back the sense of wonderment that Carter took away; he enticed us to raise our sights in a way that Ford could not; and he renewed interest in the pragmatic, albeit commercial, side of space in a way that Nixon never could.

However, what seems to be absent from Reagan's rhetoric of space is an understanding of scientific exploration of the heavens. There is no call for knowledge for knowledge's sake; there is no sense of "Let's explore to see what we can find." Rather, Reagan's vision of the commercialization of the *new frontier* first asks us to explore, then casts us as explorers, and finally remakes us into the explorers reaping the benefits of hard work—"outproducing the pants off of anybody."[19] Scientific exploration of space, however, did have a place in Reagan's vision of a renewed national defense.

THE MILITARIZATION OF SPACE

When Reagan campaigned to become president of the United States, he argued that it was important to have a strong national defense. After being elected president, Reagan continued to work to increase both the stature and the budget of the Pentagon. While he was not a warmonger, he very much believed that one could negotiate well only when dealing from a position of strength. His penchant for calling the MX missile a "peacekeeper" was indicative of this position.

It was not unusual for Reagan to give speeches geared toward increasing funds for the military. Thus, when Reagan announced that he was going to give one of those speeches on March 23, 1983, hardly an eyebrow was raised—not, at least, until the speech was over.[20] While the address was mostly concerned with procuring funds for military spending, it also focused on developing a space-bound system of defense. Dubbed "Star Wars" by the press, Reagan's call for a Strategic Defense Initiative (SDI) was a call for the militarization of space.

Militarizing space per se was not a new concept. Ever since *Sputnik I*, the Department of Defense, in conjunction with the president, had overseen the development and deployment of various types of reconnaissance satellites. Eisenhower had given the okay for the first spy satellites, Kennedy had committed us to a program of press blackouts concerning anti-satellite (ASAT) development and reconnaissance, and Johnson, Nixon, Ford, and Carter, to varying degrees, had continued our commitment to a satellite spy program.[21]

At the same time, however, that these presidents were authorizing spy satellites, they were also calling for peaceful use of space. Eisenhower, for instance, went to great lengths to constantly remind the nation and the world that our civilian space agency was oriented toward peace. Consider too that even as Kennedy pushed for ASAT development he also campaigned for a ban on nuclear weapons in space. Johnson's call for a "race for peace" is well documented, as is his campaign for an Outer Space treaty. Finally, while Carter's policies did not result in any outer space agreement, he did suggest to the Soviet Union that "we forego the opportunity to arm satellite bodies, and also . . . forego the opportunity to destroy observation satellites."[22]

According to Paul Stares, by the end of the 1970s the military use of space was "*essentially supportive* or *ancillary* to terrestrial military missions."[23] Despite predictions to the contrary, outer space had not become an arena for deploying or using weapon systems. That policy changed with Reagan's call for developing laser weapons and shields for use in or from space.

Jerry Grey has argued that Reagan's development of a Strategic Defense Initiative should not have been surprising.

By 1981, orbital space around the Earth unquestionably belonged to Soviet cosmonauts and their allies. With the escalating concern about first-strike supremacy that accompanied the breakdown of the Strategic Arms Limitation Treaty (SALT) talks, the fact that Russian military personnel were in possession of the "high ground" of space began to loom as an ominous, although still unspoken, threat to U.S. national security.[24]

Still, Reagan's speech did catch people by surprise, and as a public aspect of his space policy, his "Star Wars" policy deserves some analysis. Overall, it appears that the strategy Reagan's images employed called for the militarization of space by turning war into peace and the scientific capacity for nuclear destruction into the technological wizardry that could now save us.

A Vision of Hope

In proposing his defense initiative, Reagan used the language of space exploration: "My fellow Americans, tonight we're *launching* an effort which *holds the promise* of *changing* the *course of human history*. . . . Let me share with you a *vision* of the *future* which *offers hope*. It is that we *embark* on a *program* to *counter* the *awesome* Soviet missile threat with *measures that are defensive*" (italics added).[25]

Such images made it clear that this was a new program, one that was just getting off the ground and that might, in the future, alter history. Characteristic of Reagan's overall images, these images too take their form from historical observation—most notably from our prior space efforts. *Launching* this effort takes us back to all of our earlier launches, back to the *Mercury* experiments, the *Gemini* explorations, and the *Apollo* moon missions. The image of *changing the course of history* works to signal the realization that those launchings altered the direction of the United States.

In that the image of a Soviet threat is built into the passage, the specific historical image ignited is of the battle between *freedom* and *tyranny*, between democracy and communism.[26] Into this equation come thoughts about nuclear war, cold war, and a policy of deterrence, and about John Kennedy and his challenge to reach for the moon as well. A sense of struggle is ignited, but the image, rather than depressing, actually is uplifting.

The concept of turning the struggle between the United States and the Soviet Union into a positive vision occured as well in a set of remarks Reagan made about SDI at a National Space Club Luncheon.

The Strategic Defense Initiative has been labeled "star wars" but it isn't about war; it's about peace. It isn't about retaliation; it's about prevention. It isn't about fear; it's about hope. And in that struggle, if you'll pardon my stealing a film line: The force is with us.[27]

With simple mastery, the juxtaposition of very opposite entities creates a situation whereby out of war comes peace, from retaliation comes prevention, and from fear comes hope. Notice how one side of the equation represents a more defensive posture: war, retaliation, and fear. Notice too how the other side cultivates offense: peace, prevention, and hope. Working back and forth between these polarities, Reagan is able to transform a system of strategic defense into a system of strategic offense. SDI retains its defensive posture but is rhetorically given a place in a system of offensive strategy. As a result, SDI fits more comfortably with our ongoing offensive policy of defense—it becomes more appealing.

Scientific Saviors

Just as Reagan turned SDI into an offensive vision of hope, so too he had to alter our understanding of technology and nuclear scientists. The sort of weapons Reagan called for, after all, are the sort that could be misused were they to fall into the wrong hands. Reagan's images work to give us an alternative understanding in two ways.

First, Reagan's images attempt to turn the "mad scientist" into the "good scientist." Consider this passage from his Star Wars speech: "I call upon the scientific community in our country, those who gave us nuclear weapons, to turn their great talents now to the cause of mankind and world peace, to give us the means of rendering these nuclear weapons impotent and obsolete."[28]

Very specifically, Reagan acknowledges that the target group comprises those who brought us the atomic and neutron bombs. The emotionalism of the Manhattan Project, *Fat Man* and *Little Boy*, Nagasaki, and Hiroshima are activated in the process. We see the scientist in his white robe mixing dangerous potions that will cause death and destruction everywhere.

There is hope, however. In his vision Reagan holds out hope that these scientists might reform themselves by coming up with an antidote for their own poison. Moreover, who better to end the threat of nuclear destruction than the very people who gave it to us? The ingenuity of Reagan's vision here works precisely because of the historical oppression it ignites. A great number of our atomic scientists did feel guilty that their work on the atom bomb caused the deaths of so many innocent people. This vision, then, becomes a way of righting past wrongs. By making the commitment to discover a "nuclear antidote," the scientists can once again serve humankind and world peace. The passage is extremely compelling.

In a lesser move, Reagan's images unite scientific technology and our standard of living. He stated, "Let us turn to the very strengths in technology that spawned our great industrial base and that have given us the quality of life we enjoy today."[29] While not as emotional as the first example, this passage does conjure up an understanding of American greatness. On the one hand, infused into the passage is a sense of technology as a life-giving force. Images of test-tube babies, miracle cures, life-support systems, and the like are brought into focus. On the other hand is an enhanced quality of life: the barren parents who are now fulfilled, the cancer patient who lives comfortably, and the accident victim who comes back from the brink of death.

The passage does not, however, dwell on the technological marvels of the present age; rather, it reaches back and extols an image of a time gone by. What comes into play here is the turn-of-the-century country that was using its newfound technological (mechanical) skills to manufacture products for a whole nation of people. Still, the outcome is similar. Due to technological expertise, be it contemporary or modern, life as we know it has been improved.

Within this framework, SDI again takes on the characteristic of an offensive entity. Backed by the force of technology and scientific directive, it prompts us to consider the positive side of using space for our own, albeit military, advantage.

In both the militarization of space and the commercialization of space, Reagan emphasized the concept of the *new frontier.* With respect to commercialization, this new frontier becomes an arena in which we can repeatedly demonstrate the strength of the American character while simultaneously building the great American nation. In terms of militarization, the frontier also assumes importance as an arena in which we can preserve freedom and change the course of history while again demonstrating the strength of the American character and nation. Reagan's vision of outer space, then, is one that continuously stresses the importance of who we are as Americans.

Reagan's perspective on space gave the space program more of a raison d'être than ever before. At least for a few years, the program basked in the limelight of presidential attention, renewed commitments to exploration, the new shuttle transportation system, commercial initiatives, and "Star Wars." Then tragedy occurred. The space shuttle *Challenger* exploded seventy-three seconds after liftoff, and in killing all seven of its crew members, dampened space "spirit" and engendered criticism. The renewed vision was now in jeopardy.

NOTES

1. See Howard E. McCurdy, *The Space Station Decision* (Baltimore: Johns Hopkins University Press, 1990); Charles Murray and Catherine Bly Cox, *Apollo* (New York: Simon and Schuster, 1989); and Neil McAleer, *The Omni Space Almanac* (New York: World Almanac, 1987), for an understanding of incremental politics.

2. McCurdy, *Space Station Decision*, 41.

3. Frank B. Gibney and George J. Feldman, *The Reluctant Space-Farers: A Study in the Politics of Discovery* (New York: NAL-World, 1965), 7.

4. Ronald Reagan, "State of the Union Address," 25 Jan. 1984, *Public Papers of the Presidents of the United States, Ronald Reagan, 1984*, vol. I (Washington, D.C.: U.S. Government Printing Office, 1986), 90. (Hereafter abbreviated *PPP, RR, year*.)

5. Ronald Reagan, "Radio Address to the Nation on Commercial Space Initiatives," 21 July 1984, *PPP, RR, 1984*, vol. II (Washington, D.C.: U.S. Government Printing Office, 1986), 1071.

6. Roderick P. Hart, *Verbal Style and the Presidency* (Orlando, Fla.: Academic, 1984), 212-37.

7. Ronald Reagan, "Remarks at a White House Ceremony Commemorating the Bicentennial Year of Air and Space Flight," 7 Feb. 1983, *PPP, RR, 1983*, vol. I (Washington, D.C.: U.S. Government Printing Office, 1984), 199.

8. Ronald Reagan, "Remarks at a White House Ceremony Marking the 15th Anniversary of the Apollo 11 Lunar Landing," 20 July 1984, *PPP, RR, 1984*, II: 1067.

9. Ibid.

10. Ronald Reagan, "Remarks at the 25th Anniversary Celebration of the National Aeronautics and Space Administration," 19 Oct. 1983, *PPP, RR, 1983*, vol II (Washington, D.C.: U.S. Government Printing Office, 1984), 1481.

11. Ibid.

12. Ronald Reagan, "Remarks at the National Space Club Luncheon," 29 Mar. 1985, *PPP, RR, 1985*, vol. I (Washington, D.C.: U.S. Government Printing Office, 1988), 365.

13. Reagan, "Bicentennial Year of Air and Space Flight," *PPP, RR, 1983*, I: 198.

14. Ibid.

15. Ronald Reagan, "Remarks During a Visit to the Goddard Space Flight Center in Greenbelt, Maryland," 30 Aug. 1984, *PPP, RR, 1984*, II: 1208.

16. Reagan, "National Space Club Luncheon," *PPP, RR, 1985,* I: 365.

17. Ronald Reagan, "Radio Address to the Nation on Commercial Initiatives," 21 July 1984, *PPP, RR, 1984,* II: 1071.

18. Reagan, "Goddard Space Flight Center," *PPP, RR, 1984,* II: 1209.

19. Ibid., II: 1208.

20. Ronald Reagan, "Address to the Nation on Defense and National Security," 23 Mar. 1983, *PPP, RR, 1983,* I: 437.

21. See Paul B. Stares, *The Militarization of Space* (Ithaca, N.Y.: Cornell University Press, 1985). Stares has separate chapters devoted to Eisenhower, Kennedy, Johnson, Nixon and Ford, Carter, and Reagan, as well as discussions about spy satellites.

22. Quoted in ibid., 181.

23. Ibid., 17.

24. Jerry Grey, *Beachheads in Space: A Blueprint for the Future* (New York: MacMillan, 1983), 38.

25. Reagan, "Defense and National Security," *PPP, RR, 1983,* I: 443.

26. For further explanation, see Richard Fox and T. Jackson Lears, eds., *The Culture of Consumption* (New York: Pantheon, 1983), 195.

27. Reagan, "National Space Club Luncheon," *PPP, RR, 1985,* I: 363.

28. Reagan, "Defense and National Security," *PPP, RR, 1983,* I: 442.

29. Ibid., 443.

Chapter Five

Back to the Future

On January 28, 1986, the space shuttle *Challenger* lifted off on its most momentous mission. Aboard was a top-notch crew of seven astronauts, Dick Scobee, Mike Smith, Judy Resnik, Ellison Onizuka, Ron McNair, Greg Jarvis, and "teacher in space" Christa McAuliffe. Aside from its scientific aspect, the mission had two additional, sociopolitical, dimensions. First, it was going to relay the importance of teachers as "preservers and protectors of our heritage." As Reagan had told the finalists of the Teacher in Space Project, "You save our past from being consumed by forgetfulness, and our future from being engulfed in ignorance."[1] At the same time, having a civilian teacher aboard was intended to convey the fact that space exploration really had become routine.

Unfortunately, the mission failed to achieve either of its objectives. Seventy-three seconds after liftoff, a faulty O-ring broke, causing the shuttle to burst into flames and explode. The civilian teacher never made it to space, and the *new frontier* was now a question mark in many minds. As the first in-air disaster for the United States, it forced leaders and public alike to rethink the tenor of the space program.

For all those frustrated with the space program, the *Challenger* disaster became a symbol of bureaucracy gone bad. Amid employee resignations and organizational shakedowns, rumors surfaced that NASA's public relations machine had been overly concerned with image, that the agency as a whole had been too preoccupied with protecting its space contracts and space jobs, and that consequently the organization had put the safety of its space program over the safety of the astronauts.[2] It took nearly three years to get the organization back on track.

In the meantime, President Ronald Reagan, and later President George Bush, sought to lift our spirits and understanding of the space program. Both presented visions of space that reached back to the rhetoric of John Kennedy and yet pushed us forward into the future. Understanding how this was accomplished is the subject of this chapter.

REAGAN RENEWS

Reagan's pre-*Challenger* space metaphors set the tone of his post-*Challenger* rhetoric. We were still asked to keep moving forward to greatness and to keep sight of the *new frontier.* However, there occurred a slight change. No longer were we the frontiersmen working and thriving on the new frontier, but rather, we became the first pioneers seeking to discover the new land.

Summoning the Pioneers

Reagan changed our identity from frontiersmen to pioneers in several moves. First of all, he argued that the astronauts themselves were pioneers. In a speech commemorating the first anniversary of the *Challenger* explosion, for instance, Reagan made such a claim:

They know that exploration has its risks. They know that with adventure, goes danger. They know all this, but they also know something far more important: something about the spirit and sense of joy that have kept man reaching through the ages to grasp for the limits of his universe and beyond that, despite hardships and peril.[3]

The passage easily conjures up a vision of the first pioneers who dared cross into uncharted territory. It takes us back to the time when the thrill of adventure was moderated by the threat of danger. Into this framework these images ask us to place not only the "*Challenger* Seven," but all our astronauts. We are asked to think of those astronauts as individuals who sought to go beyond the edges of the universe, both literally and figuratively.

Overall, the identification forged in this passage works because of the kind of historical and everyday experiences on which it draws. The very word *pioneer* conjures up both textbook and television visions of explorers, scouts, cowboys, Indians, and the cavalry. Even more, however, than drawing attention to the mere picture of pioneers like Daniel Boone and Davy Crockett, these images call our attention to what lies beneath the act of pioneering, the pioneering spirit.

As a result, we needed not know any actual pioneers in order to understand who the astronauts were. Rather, we merely needed to know the thrill of an adventure modified by fear in order to understand. Nearly all of us have at some point enacted the role of pioneer, whether it be beginning a new job, trying a new restaurant, or just making a commitment to take a ride on a roller coaster. Merging the sense of excitement with the sense of fear, this image compels us to think of the astronauts as people who, like us, tried new things.

As Reagan's images work to supplant a new understanding of the "*Challenger* Seven," they also work to offer a new vision of ourselves and our program. Like the astronauts, we the people of the United States and our space program, are whisked back into a pioneering posture. Consider a passage from Reagan's speech on the eve of the *Challenger* explosion: "We've grown used to wonders. . . . It's hard to dazzle us. But for 25 years the U.S. space program has been doing just that. We've grown used to the idea of space, and perhaps we forget that we've only just begun."[4]

Lodged amid a contradiction between wonder and routine, the images of the passage incite us to think differently about the space program. Once again our experience with the space program is brought into play. We are reminded of the shrinking audiences who now come to witness a space launch and of the television networks that only reluctantly interrupt daytime soap operas to bring us the launch. We are reminded of Carter's space policy and the overall justification of moving toward a space shuttle. We are reminded as well about the high

American level of expectation and the difficulty of "wowing" us with new things.

Into this bit of reminiscing, Reagan placed our space program. With a bit of juxtapositioning, Reagan found a way to make the routine, ordinary space program special. With a bit of mastery, he turned it into something that has been "wowing" us all along. That we did not even realize this speaks to its ability to "wow." Moreover, in revealing this aspect of the space program, Reagan paved the way for a new understanding: We're just beginning.

Moreover, having taken us back to the beginning, back to the pioneers on the edge of the frontier, Reagan could then, as before, push us forward. "Go forward America, reach for the stars,"[5] he asserted during his State of the Union address. "We must continue," he stated at the annual dinner of the Conservative Political Action conference. "Other brave Americans must go now where they so valiantly tried to lead—a fitting place, I've always thought, for Americans: 'the stars and beyond.'"[6] "This has been a difficult passage of America," Reagan stated upon receiving the report on the *Challenger* accident, "but we will go on—America has a claim to stake on the future."[7]

Moving forward, pushing ahead, and continuing are all images that, as before the *Challenger* accident, said much about the American character. Character is still a motivating force, but so too is that pioneering spirit. Indeed, we see this pioneering spirit even more clearly after the launch of the shuttle *Discovery* nearly three years after the *Challenger* explosion. A few days before the launch occurred, Reagan stated:

You can delay our long trek to greatness, but you cannot halt it. Soon the world will be watching as five brave Americans lift off from Earth. America is going to space again—and we are going there to stay. Our early settlers knew great risks and made great sacrifices, but with their sacrifices, they moved the frontier forward and built a great nation. Neither can we stand still, nor be content, and we are not afraid. Ill fortune can slow us down, but it cannot stop us.[8]

Here is the vision of the pioneer moving forward regardless of the costs or the obstacles. The pioneering character is featured: adventure mixing with fear, risks merging with sacrifices, frontiers pushed back, and great nations built—as is the renewed vision of the space program that Reagan worked so hard to establish before *Challenger* exploded. After *Discovery*, we were back to the *new frontier*.

This was not entirely true, however. Two years after the *Challenger* tragedy, Reagan's rhetoric began to sound very much like his pre-*Challenger* rhetoric. Once *Discovery* lifted off, we were still beginners, but at least we were back. There was, however, one significant change in Reagan's vision of space. Whereas before there was a clear link between commercialization, NASA, and space exploration, now that link was dissolved. Instead, there was now a clear link between commercialization, space, and private industry.

Pioneering and Commercializing

Reagan visualized two different roles in outer space, one for NASA and one for private industry. On a pragmatic level, it is possible that the continual delays in bringing the shuttle fleet back up to full speed after *Challenger*, plus a backlog of commercial satellites, convinced Reagan to pare down some of NASA's expectations. On another level, it is also possible that Reagan came to the conclusion that strong commercial initiatives needed strong frontiersmen, not beginning pioneers.

The call for a dual outer space initiative came on the heels of the final report on the *Challenger* accident. In a speech on the future of the space program, Reagan stated:

NASA and the shuttles will continue to lead the way, breaking new ground, pioneering new technology, pushing back the frontiers. It has been determined, however, that NASA will no longer be in the business of launching private satellites. . . . NASA will keep America on the leading edge of change; the private sector will take over from there and ensure a robust, balanced, safe program.[9]

Stripping commercial interests from the program of outer space exploration served to remind the nation that NASA's job is exploration, not business. Simultaneously, it reminded us that exploration is risky and hazardous while business is robust and safe. The move made in these images is one that functions to exonerate business from any liability or responsibility for space disasters. Without its business aspect, NASA alone became responsible for any difficulties that might arise.

All told, the move from frontiersmen to pioneer and from space commercialization to space and commercialization probably hurt NASA more than it helped the agency. While it gave NASA the opportunity to focus squarely on outer space exploration, it also eroded its primary base of support—private industry. As a result, by the time Reagan left office, the space program was not really in any better shape than it was when he first took power. True, it had a vision, but its sense of mission was fading as its base of support began to disappear.

BUSH MAKES A COMMITMENT

Even as Reagan was turning us back into pioneers and setting space initiatives for both NASA and the private sector, the viability of his vision was losing legislative attention and support. The difficulties that NASA was experiencing, the long delay between the *Challenger* disaster and the flight of *Discovery*, the continual demands for moon probes and other costly expeditions, and a growing deficit all challenged Reagan's visionary attitude. Simply seeking a challenge was no longer a good enough basis for a national space program.

John Logsdon, director of George Washington University's Space Policy Institute, argued in October 1988 that what was needed was "a purposeful, well funded, coherent program." NASA advisor Alan Ladwig agreed, and urged a "national commitment to space." "It's up to the White House and Congress to lead. It's not NASA's job anymore."[10] Whether George Bush would make such a national commitment was unknown. What was known was that as head of the president's Space Council, and as a presidential candidate, Bush had supported both aspects of Reagan's space policy. NASA officials and space enthusiasts hoped that Bush would do something to etch out a major commitment to space.

The Vision

An attempt at that commitment came on July 20, 1989, during a celebration commemorating the twentieth anniversary of landing on the moon. Straight to the point, Bush stated:

In order for the United States to lead the world in colonizing space, I'm not proposing a 10-year plan like Apollo. I'm proposing a long range continuing commitment: first, for the coming decade, for the 1990s, Space Station Freedom, our critical next step in all our space endeavors. And next, for the new century, back to the moon, back to the future and, this time, back to stay. And then a journey into tomorrow, a journey to another planet, a manned mission to Mars. Each mission should and will lay the groundwork for the next.[11]

These thoughts were the very ones that space enthusiasts and NASA officials were waiting to hear. President Bush was laying out a long-range commitment to space which would continue beyond his presidency. Unfortunately, the images in which Bush cast his space directives were not overly concrete, and as a result, they were difficult to pin down. Indeed, it is difficult to understand exactly what Bush had in store for the space program.

Some facts do emerge. There is something in his message about finishing the space station. There is also something about going back to the moon. In addition, there is something about the future that is intermingled with the idea of Mars. However, the thoughts are fuzzy. Designed to move us forward toward the future, then backward to our previous outer space exploits, and then forward again to a more tenable position, the images founder. the images appear to be Reaganesque in form, and yet they have no life, no history. There is, in other words, not much substance beneath *journey into tomorrow*, save for the title of a box office movie, *Back to the Future*. The attempt at vision fails.

The Plan

Later in the address, Bush worked to give some direction to his vision. He stated, ''We cannot take the next giant leap for mankind tomorrow unless we take a single step today."[12] Unlike his "visionary images," this reordering of the words Neil Armstrong said when stepping onto the moon does motivate us to accept Bush's plan.

The reason, of course, is that this statement taps into historical experience—the lunar landing—and, at the same time, into the social experience of putting a process into place. The images here suggest that we must walk before we can run, that we must take things slowly, and that we must progress in a step-by-step manner. Just as the experience of *one thing at a time* makes common sense, so too it ought to make sense in relation to the space program.

This sense of process came out as well when Bush directed Vice President Dan Quayle to lead the Space Council "in determining specifically what's needed for the next round of exploration, the necessary money, manpower and material, the feasibility of international cooperation, and develop realistic timetables, milestones along the way."[13] What emerges here is a very specific set of procedures for investigating the possibility of outer space exploration. Bush proposes his vision, next it is studied, then a set of recommendations emerges, followed by timetables, and so on. In comparison to his "vision" of outer space exploration, this concept is specific and concrete. One image, however, detracts here. While the *next round* fits in with the language of process, it also shares a conceptual heritage with such things as negotiations and game playing. On the one hand, then, Bush is suggesting that his vision of space exploration is open to negotiations; on the other hand, it is part of a game. With such an ambiguous concept thrown into the overall image of process, the overall thrust of Bush's space vision is unclear.

Procedurally, the steps for a strong space program appear to be in place. However gracefully, Bush has acknowledged that we ought to build our permanent space station, go back to the moon, and then think about a mission to Mars. It is a comprehensive program in terms of what it should accomplish, and yet it is not concrete enough in its rationale. There is no basis for justifying the program, and there is no vision as to how it will become a part of our national priorities. As of this writing, it is too early to adequately evaluate Bush's space position. However, if we make assessments based on his rhetoric so far, it is doubtful that under Bush the space program is going to thrive.

NOTES

1. Ronald Reagan, "Remarks to the Finalists in the Teacher in Space Project," 26 June 1985, *Public Papers of the Presidents of the United States, Ronald Reagan, 1985,* vol. I (Washington, D.C.: U.S. Government Printing Office, 1988), 825. (Hereafter abbreviated *PPP, RR, year.*)

2. H. L. Goodall, *Casing a Promised Land* (Carbondale: Southern Illinois University Press, 1989) especially chapters 3 and 4.

3. Ronald Reagan, "Remarks to Employees of the National Aeronautics and Space Administration on the First Anniversary of the Explosion of the Space Shuttle *Challenger,*" 28 Jan. 1987, *PPP, RR, 1987,* vol. I (Washington, D.C.: U.S. Government Printing Office, 1989), 80.

4. Ronald Reagan, "Address to the Nation on the Explosion of the Space Shuttle *Challenger,*" 28 Jan. 1986, *PPP, RR, 1986,* vol. I (Washington, D.C.: U.S. Government Printing Office, 1988), 95.

5. Ronald Reagan, "State of the Union Address," 4 Feb. 1986, *PPP, RR, 1986,* I: 125.

6. Ronald Reagan, "Remarks at the Annual Dinner of the Conservative Political Action Conference." 30 Jan. 1986, *PPP, RR, 1986,* I: 104.

7. Ronald Reagan, "Remarks on Receiving the Final Report of the Presidential Commission on the Space Shuttle *Challenger* Accident," 9 June 1986, *PPP, RR, 1986,* I: 736.

8. "Shuttle Launch," *Duluth News Tribune,* 23 Sept. 1988, 5A.

9. Ronald Reagan, "Statement on the Building of a Fourth Shuttle Orbiter and the Future of the Space Program," 15 Aug. 1986, *PPP, RR, 1986,* vol. II (Washington, D.C.: U.S. Government Printing Office, 1988), 1111.

10. Quoted in *Time,* 10 Oct. 1988, 25.

11. Quoted in "Bush Asks Renewal of Space Program," *Minneapolis Star Tribune* 21 July, 1989, 1A.

12. Ibid.

13. Ibid.

Chapter Six

Thirty-odd Years of
Metaphoric Guidance

Throughout this text my emphasis has been on presidents and their visions of outer space exploration. In particular, my interest was in understanding the relationship between a president's metaphorical images and his perspective on space exploration. Having explored some thirty years of metaphorical guidance, it is now possible to make some global assessments about the U.S. program of space exploration.

Overall, this chapter contends that the problems with the space program are both directly and indirectly tied to the way in which presidents have talked about it, and that the consequences of this rhetoric on the space program have been costly. In particular, it argues that as of yet, no president has been able to overcome the fundamental contradiction between space "exploration" and space "use" to forge an appropriate vision of space exploration.

THE PERSPECTIVES REVISITED

Back in 1957, Dwight Eisenhower had the right idea about the space program. From within his managerial pespective, Eisenhower saw space as important in its own right. He wanted the United States to have a space program not because the Soviet Union had one or because we needed one to feel better about ourselves, but because the fundamental idea of outer space exploration was important. As a person familiar with bureaucratic processes and with the big picture, Eisenhower came the closest of all the presidents to forging a national purpose and identity for the space program.

Hard as he tried, however, Eisenhower was unable to change and rechannel the fears and concerns expressed by representatives of the press and public. He was unable to keep the space program from becoming a means to an end rather than an end in itself. *Sputnik I* and Soviet domination were on everybody's mind, it seemed, and Eisenhower could not change that. His managerial rhetoric and *plan* perspective were unable to establish a vision of a strong space program that could, at that time, compare with the one the Soviet Union seemed to have in place.

It is entirely possible that no rhetoric would have soothed the space frenzy created by the Soviet *Sputniks* except a total race posture. Nonetheless, as history points up, even John Kennedy's *race* perspective was inadequate.

Acting out of a politically expedient framework, Kennedy entered the United States in a "crash program" of space catch-up. His stirring images of the struggle between *tyranny* and *freedom* helped assert the necessity of such a race. For a while, Kennedy's vision loomed large. The crash program mobilized our efforts, and the *Mercury* and *Gemini* missions began to get underway. We were seemingly committed to a national program of outer space exploration, or was it merely a commitment to a *race*?

Neither Kennedy's *race* perspective nor the way in which it played into the struggle between *tyranny* and *freedom* were strong enough to set a long-range tone for the space program. Where his perspective failed was, first, in its short-term nature. Races come and go: They may last for a number of weeks, and they may emerge time and time again, but characteristically, races are short-term. Like all races, ours with the Soviet Union would end.

More important, however, is the fact that while Kennedy asserted that we were racing with the Soviet Union, his images actually depicted more of a struggle or battle. There is, of course, a sense of struggle that underlies a race, and yet what is missing from Kennedy's rhetoric is the sense of competition out of which races are truly born. Kennedy was unable to picture our tryst with the Soviet Union in a competitive way, and as a result, the *race* perspective was not satisfying.

Lyndon Johnson was able to use the *race* metaphor in a more successful way. He was able to demonstrate that for the first decade of space efforts, the United States and the Soviet Union had been engaged in a kind of "competitive spacemanship." Like Kennedy, however, Johnson could not avoid stressing the *struggle* side of the *race*, and as a result, his *race* became a kind of *war*. That Johnson's images were riddled with a fundamental contradiction between world unity and world division, as well as being devoid of fiscal responsibility, also hindered the establishment of a sound program of space exploration.

Out of the first decade of space exploration came two concepts: one of space and one of exploration. While the *race* perspective did get the American people thinking about space, it failed to get them thinking about space exploration.

Space and exploration were united at the beginning of the second decade of the space program. In merging the concept of wonderment with the notion of *use*, Nixon was able to forge a strong rationale for space exploration and utilization. His images, in fact, demonstrated that these two processes came from the same foundation, and that both were equally important in projecting an understanding of the space program. Where Nixon's images failed, however, was in their inability to forge a sense of individual participation in the process of space exploration. Nixon's images, in other words, were geared toward thinking rather than doing.

Ironically, during his short term as vice-president and president, Gerald Ford was able to forge a more active vision of the space program even as he sought to make it more *routine*. With Ford's perspective came a renewed sense of awe and respect for endeavors of exploration, especially with respect to the possibility that exploration could result in a better world. Unfortunately, the experiences into which Ford tapped in projecting his vision were not common nor substantive enough to make a convincing case. More than anything, Ford's overall image revealed the shortcomings of space exploration in relation to making a better life.

Jimmy Carter's goal, from the perspective of his images, was to counter the shortcomings of space exploration and to make the space program accountable to the American public. From within the perspective of a financial advisor, Carter asked us to reconceptualize our space program in terms of costs and benefits. Carter was correct in his assessment that space exploration needed to be balanced by financial expediency, yet that vision alone was not enough to sustain the space program. Without a corresponding sense of wonderment, the space program failed to become part of our national priorities and was transformed into a kind of grind.

Ronald Reagan renewed the space program as it entered its third decade of existence. Reagan's image of a space program *standing tall* tapped into the most basic of human and American experiences; it forged an intriguing and palatable sense of mission for outer space exploration. However, even in Reagan's vision, space exploration was only a means to an end. On the one hand, it existed as a *character-building frontier*, a proving ground on which all Americans could demonstrate their worth as citizens. On the other hand, it existed as a *commercial frontier* whereby the great American nation could continue to reap economic greatness. As a result, it was Reagan's perspective on space that renewed Americans and America, not a commitment to outer space exploration.

George Bush has made a commitment to outer space exploration, or at least to a long-range plan of space exploration. His call for a permanent space station, a moon base, and an expedition to Mars indeed should be viewed differently in the context of past short-term, one-shot objectives. Still, Bush's vision is incomplete. Nowhere in his rhetoric is there a coherent understanding of why space exploration is important, save for the necessity of a step-by-step approach. Nowhere in his rhetoric is there a coherent explanation as to how space exploration can be used. Without a more comprehensive vision, Bush's vision cannot revive the space program.

MOVING AHEAD

Exploring outer space ought to be a national priority for the United States. It is okay if we want to host a space race with other countries, make space exploration routine and cost-efficient, or be the first to people an outer space outpost. However, first we must have some more fundamental reasons for going into space; we must find the images that explain how and why this exploration is vitally important, both spiritually and pragmatically.

To date, our presidents have been unable to merge space exploration and space use together in such a way as to fashion a strong U.S. space program. That merger cannot happen until we make a commitment to a space program as a space program, and not as a means to some social or political end. Consider again what has happened with the space program. Kennedy used the space program as a way to preserve national prestige and freedom, while Johnson turned it into a vehicle for achieving peace on earth. Ford made space a tool for overcoming the shame of Watergate, while Carter used it as a way to better think about concerns on earth. Reagan, of course, used space as means for economic and spiritual growth. Only Eisenhower, Nixon, and Bush made a commitment to having a strong space program, and out of these three, only two, Eisenhower and Bush, envisioned a long-range plan.

Beyond this commitment, our presidents need to be able to draw on common resources in the American experience. The more common the image, the greater its base of support and appeal. The historical, social, and physical experiences evoked in Kennedy's rhetoric as well as in that of Ford and Reagan stand as excellent examples; those that emerge in the rhetoric of Johnson, Carter, and Bush serve as examples of experiences to avoid.

Metaphor is a linguistic phenomenon that functions to draw upon, exploit, and overcome the many contradictions in our experiences. Because by their very nature metaphors are capable of overcoming contradictions, they become the perfect means for altering our understanding of our space program, and the best way for merging space exploration and space use.

In revealing past metaphorical perspectives, this study will provide impetus to new ones. With the strengths and weaknesses of each presidential perspective assessed, it will become possible to envision what future perspectives must do. We need, for instance, a perspective that will raise our sights (Ford), renew our sense of self (Reagan), give us a sense of challenge (Kennedy), establish a base of wonderment (Nixon), call for a long-range commitment (Bush), lay out a procedure for achieving such a commitment (Eisenhower), and demonstrate the many benefits of a space program (Carter). Nothing short of a total vision will change the current direction of the space program.

Chronology

1957

Oct. 4   Soviet Union launches the first satellite, *Sputnik I.*

Oct. 9   President Eisenhower responds to *Sputnik:* "The U.S. has never considered its space program as a race; merely an engagement on our part to put up a vehicle of this kind."[1]

Nov. 3   Soviet Union launches the second satellite, *Sputnik II.* It carries a dog named Laika.

Nov. 7   Eisenhower addresses the American people on science in national security: "Certainly we need to feel a high sense of urgency. But this does not mean that we should mount our charger and try to ride off in all directions at once."[2]

Dec. 6   U.S. rocket *Vanguard* explodes on the launch pad.

1958

Jan. 31   United States successfully launches a satellite, *Explorer I.* Eisenhower reminds the public that "the launching is part of our country's participation in the International Geophysical Year."[3]

Mar. 17   U.S. rocket *Vanguard* successfully puts a small satellite into orbit.

Mar. 26   Eisenhower releases his Science Advisory Committee's report entitled, "Introduction to Outer Space."

"Every person has the opportunity to share through understanding in the adventures which lie ahead."[4]

Apr. 2   NASA (National Aeronautics and Space Administration) is proposed. Eisenhower states that "an imaginative and well conceived space program must be given high priority and a sound organization provided to carry it out."[5]

May 15   Soviet Union launches *Sputnik III*.

July 29   Eisenhower signs the National Aeronautics and Space Act of 1958, declaring that it will "equip the United States for leadership in the space age."[6]

1959

Jan. 3   Soviet Union launches the first moon probe, *Luna 3*.

Jan. 28   Eisenhower attempts to convince the press and the nation that our space program is "a matter for pride on the part of America, and not a constant—well, hangdog attitude of humiliation."[7]

Mar. 3   United States launches space probe *Pioneer*. Eisenhower states that it "marks yet another major step in scientific space exploration" which "should provide important additions to man's knowledge of the universe."[8]

Apr. 9   The first U. S. astronauts, the "Magnificent Seven," are selected for Project Mercury (M. Scott Carpenter, L. Gordon Cooper, John H. Glenn, Jr., Virgil I. Grissom, Wally M. Schirra, Jr., Alan B. Shepard, Jr., and Donald K. Slayton).

May 28   Two chimps, Able and Baker, are recovered alive after a flight in a U.S. Jupiter rocket.

Aug. 3   Eisenhower reminds the nation that our scientists "are catching up as fast as they can," and asks the public to "remember that this is a period of transition. You cannot 'off with the old' immediately, and go all to the new until you have tried it out."[9]

Sept. 12   Soviet probe *Luna 2* is the first robot probe, or unmanned space vehicle, to impact the moon.

Oct. 4   Soviet probe *Luna 3* radios back the first photos of the far side of the moon.

Oct. 21   Eisenhower transfers the Army Ballistic Missile Agency to NASA "to strengthen the national space effort and provide for America's changing requirements in this field."[10]

Oct. 22   Eisenhower responds to questions of U.S. delinquency in competing with the Soviets in space: "I know this: Our plan is a positive one, and I see no reason for thinking of it merely as competition with somebody else. It is something we intend to do."[11]

1960

Jan. 26   Eisenhower argues that U.S. international prestige is not at stake. He states, "In the actual examination of these two programs, I think we've got a pretty good record."[12]

Feb. 3   Eisenhower professes confusion about the space "race": "I am always a little bit amazed about this business of catching up. What you want is enough, a thing that is adequate. . . . Therefore, you are not talking about racing them in finding the particular items or in naming the particular course that you are going to run in this race; you work out a proper and an appropriate plan of scientific exploration, and you follow it positively, rather than trying to follow along behind somebody else."[13]

Apr. 1   United States launches its first weather satellite, *Tiros I*. Eisenhower states, "Once again, many elements of our scientific, technological and industrial communities have cooperated in the further development of our national program in space exploration under NASA's leadership."[14]

May 15   Soviet Union launches a five-ton space capsule carrying life support equipment and a dummy human into earth orbit.

July 29   U.S. *Mercury* test failure on the launch pad.

Aug. 12   United States launches first passive communications satellite, *Echo 1*.

Aug. 15   Eisenhower inspects the capsule retrieved from the satellite *Discoverer XIII*. He states that "this is another incident in a remarkable series of accomplishments that show how rapidly America has forged far ahead into worthwhile exploration of space."[15]

Aug. 17   Eisenhower recounts the U.S. achievements in space, stating that "the events of the past weeks have demonstrated beyond all doubt the vigor, capabilities and leadership of the United States in the conquest of the frontiers of science and technology and in particular, in the exploration and utilization of space."[16]

Aug. 19   Soviet Union recovers a capsule with two female dogs, Belka and Strelka, still alive.

Nov. 8   John F. Kennedy is elected president of the United States.

1961

Jan. 31   U.S. chimp, Ham, successfully completes a suborbital flight in a *Mercury* capsule.

Feb. 15   Kennedy acknowledges that the United States is behind in space: "It is a matter of great concern."[17]

Apr. 12   Soviet Union launches *Vostok 1*. Cosmonaut Yuri Gagarin becomes the first human to orbit the earth. Kennedy tells reporters, "The news will be worse before it is better, and it will be some time before we catch up."[18]

Apr. 25   Kennedy amends the Aeronautics and Space Act to make the vice president—Lyndon B. Johnson—head of the Space Council. He calls it a "key step toward moving the United States into its proper place in the space race."[19]

May 5   U.S. launches *Mercury 3* flight; astronaut Alan Shepard is kept aloft for fifteen minutes. "We are proud of the efforts," Kennedy states. "We have a long way to go in the field of space. We are behind.

But we are working hard and we are going to increase our effort.''[20]

May 25   Kennedy sets the goal of landing astronauts on the moon and bringing them home again. ''Now it is time to take longer strides—time for a great new American enterprise—time for this nation to take a clearly leading role in space achievement.''[21]

July 21   United States launches *Mercury 4;* Virgil Grissom accomplishes the second U.S. suborbital flight.

Aug. 6   Soviet Union launches *Vostok* 2. The second Soviet cosmonaut orbits the earth.

Nov. 18   Kennedy defends goal of lunar landing: ''I do not believe that we want to permit the Soviet Union to dominate space, with all that it might mean to our peace and security in the coming years.''[22]

Nov. 29   U.S. chimp, Enos, makes a two-orbit flight in a Mercury capsule.

1962

Feb. 20   U.S. launches *Mercury 6.* John Glenn becomes the first American to orbit the earth. Kennedy calls it a ''magnificent achievement'' and ''a victory of technology and the human spirit.''[23]

Mar. 7   First U.S. orbiting solar observatory *(OSOL-1)* starts detailed survey of the sun from space.

Apr. 26   With Britain, United States launches the first international satellite, *Ariel I.*

May 24   United States launches *Mercury 7.*

July 10   U.S. communications satellite *Telstar 1* inaugurates live transatlantic television transmissions.

July 22   Attempted launch of U.S. space probe *Mariner 1* fails.

Aug. 11   Soviet Union launches *Vostok 3.*

Aug. 12   Soviet Union launches *Vostok 4.*

Aug. 27   United States successfully launches space probe *Mariner 2.*

Sept. 12   Kennedy defends goal of lunar landing: "No nation which expects to be the leader of other nations can expect to stay behind in this race for space." "This generation does not intend to founder in the backwash of the coming age of space. We mean to be a part of it—we mean to lead it."[24]

Oct. 3   United States launches *Mercury 8*. Kennedy calls the launch a "milestone" which "comes as the direct result of our redoubled effort in this scientific venture."

Dec. 10   United States space probe *Mariner 2* becomes the first successful interplanetary craft by detailing conditions on Venus.

1963

May 15   United States launches *Mercury 9*. Kennedy calls it an "extraordinary feat which has pushed the experience of man a good deal further in many ways than it has been."[25]

June 14   Soviet Union launches *Vostok 5*.

June 16   Soviet Union launches *Vostok 6*. It carries the first female cosmonaut into space.

July 26   U.S. *Syncom 2* becomes the first operational geostationary communications satellite.

Oct. 10   Kennedy presents the Collier Trophy to the first U.S. astronauts: "Some may only dimly perceive where we are going and what is going to happen. They may not feel that this is of the greatest priority to our country."[26]

Nov. 22   John F. Kennedy is assassinated in Dallas, Texas. Lyndon B. Johnson takes the presidential oath.

1964

Jan. 8   Johnson releases a statement about his space policy: "We must assure our preeminence in the peaceful exploration of outer space, focusing on an expedition to the moon in this decade—in cooperation with other powers if possible, alone if necessary."[27]

Jan. 29   U.S. rocket *Saturn I* launches a 37,000-pound satellite.

Johnson calls it a "giant step forward for the United States space effort."[28]

June 19   Johnson tours Edwards Air Force Base. He calls the men and women who serve in the U.S. space program the "sentries of peace and the servants of progress."[29]

July 31   U.S. moon probe *Ranger 7* hits its target and takes thousands of close-up photos of the moon before crashing.

Sept. 15   Johnson inspects the space facilities at Cape Kennedy. He tells NASA officials, "We cannot be the leader of the world and the follower in space."[30]

Nov. 3   Johnson is elected president of the United States.

1965

Feb. 25   Johnson briefs officials at NASA: "Our purpose is not, and I think all of you realize never will be, just national prestige. Our purpose remains firmly fixed on the fixed objective of peace. The frontier of space is a frontier that we believe all mankind can and should explore together for peaceful purposes."[31]

Mar. 18   Soviet Union launches *Voskhod 2*. Cosmonaut Alexei Leonov becomes the first human to walk in space.

Mar 20   Johnson tells reporters that "it was really a mistake to regard space exploration as a contest which can be tallied on any box score."[32]

Mar. 23   United States launches *Gemini 3*. Johnson states that "the historic flight today is a further measure of the unlimited role man has to play in the exploration and peaceful use of the endless frontier of space."[33]

Apr. 6   United States satellite *Early Bird* (*Intelsat 1*) becomes the first commercial communications satellite.

June 3   United States launches *Gemini 4*. Astronaut Edward White becomes the first U.S. spacewalker. Johnson remarks: "What you have done will never be forgotten. We can hope and we do pray that the time will come when all men of all nations will join together to explore space together, and walk side by side toward peace."[34]

July 29   Johnson reviews pictures of Mars taken by U.S. space probe *Mariner 4*. "Mankind's progress toward the distant stars of peace and reason must not, and shall not, be either delayed or diverted by those who would cast the shadow of fear across its path and have it fall in the darkness of war."[35]

Aug. 21   United States launches *Gemini 5*. Eight days later, Johnson telephones his congratulations: "You have certainly proved, I think, once and for all that man has a place in the exploration of the great frontier of space. . . . The one thing that we are all working for, and really our only purpose in space, is peace in the world."[36]

Aug. 23   Johnson instructs the Department of Defense to immediately proceed with the development of a manned orbiting laboratory.

Dec. 4   United States launches *Gemini 7*. Johnson states: "Once again, two brave Americans have carried the quest for knowledge to the threshold of space. Their voyage will be a continuous reminder that the peaceful conquest of space is the only form of conquest in which modern man can proudly and profitably engage."[37]

Dec. 15   United States launches *Gemini 6-A*. Johnson states: "You have all moved us one step higher on the stairway to the moon. . . . Our efforts in space will take us not only to the moon but, by increasing our knowledge of technology and the world around us, to a better life for all."[38]

1966

Feb. 1   Soviet Union space probe *Luna 9* lands an instrument capsule on the moon.

Mar. 16   United States launches *Gemini 8*. Astronauts Neil Armstrong and Dave Scott achieve first docking in space with an unmanned *Agena* target vehicle. Johnson asserts: "We haven't wiped out all the deficiencies in our program yet, but we have caught up and we are pulling ahead. . . . We intend to land the first man on the surface of the moon and we intend to do this in the decade of the sixties."[39]

Apr. 3   Soviet Union space probe *Luna 10* enters lunar orbit to become the moon's first satellite.

May 7   Johnson calls for a treaty governing the exploration of celestial bodies. "Just as the United States is striving to help achieve peace on earth, we want to do what we can to insure that explorations of the moon and other celestial bodies will be for peaceful purposes only."[40]

June 2   Johnson comments on the landing of U.S. moon probe *Surveyor I* on the Ocean of Storms: "Overnight the eyes of *Surveyor I* have become the eyes of the world on the moon. Another exciting chapter in the peaceful exploration of the universe is open for men to read and share."[41]

June 3   United States launches *Gemini 9.*

July 18   United States launches *Gemini 10.*

Aug. 14   U.S. moon probe *Orbiter 1* enters lunar orbit to become the second moon satellite.

Sept. 12   United States launches *Gemini 11.*

Nov. 11   United States launches final *Gemini* mission, number 12.

Nov. 23   Johnson concludes the *Gemini* space program and introduces the *Apollo* program. He states, "The splendid performance of man and machine in Gemini has been a product of the American system at its best. . . . Apollo will make America truly a space-faring Nation."[42]

1967

Jan. 27   Three astronauts, Virgil Grissom, Edward White, and Roger Chaffee, are killed in a fire in an *Apollo* space-craft during a pre-flight test. Johnson sends his condolences: "Three valiant young men have given their lives in the Nation's service. We mourn this great loss. Our hearts go out to their families."[43] Johnson also presides over the signing of the Treaty on Outer Space. "We have never succeeded in freeing our planet from the implements of war. But if we cannot yet achieve this goal here on earth, we can at least keep the virus from spreading."[44]

Feb. 11   Johnson releases "The Space Program in the Post-Apollo Period," a report compiled by his Science Advisory Committee.

June 14   United States launches space probe *Mariner 5.*

Oct. 10   Johnson puts the Outer Space Treaty into force. "Space is a frontier that is common to all mankind and it should be explored and conquered by humanity acting in concert."[45]

Nov. 9   United States successfully launches the rocket to be used in all Apollo missions, *Saturn V.*

Nov. 10   United States releases first full-color photos of earth from space.

1968

July 15   Johnson calls for an international Astronaut Assistance and Return Agreement: "A divided world can and must overcome its differences."[46]

Oct. 1   Johnson celebrates NASA's tenth anniversary. "In the years ahead—as in the past decade—our foremost motive is to make men wiser and life on earth more meaningful."[47]

Oct. 11   United States launches *Apollo 7.* Johnson states: "The path to the moon takes courage, ability, and devotion to our goals. You are making a major stride on this star-studded way."[48]

Nov. 5   Richard M. Nixon is elected president of the United States.

Dec. 7   United States launches the first successful large-scale orbiting astronomical observatory *(OSO-2)*, to investigate the ultraviolet region of outer space.

Dec. 21   United States launches *Apollo 8*. Johnson states, ''The visions of the past are coming closer and closer to becoming the amazing achievements of the present.''[49]

1969

Jan. 14   Soviet spacecrafts *Soyuz 4* and *Soyuz 5* become the first to link up and transfer crews in space.

Feb. 13   Richard Nixon empowers a Space Task Group headed by Vice President Spiro Agnew to prepare a ''definitive recommendation on the direction of the U.S. post-Apollo space program.''[50]

Mar. 3   United States launches *Apollo 9*. Ten days later, Nixon states: ''The epic flight of Apollo 9 will be recorded in history as ten days that thrilled the world. You . . . have shown the world that man and his technological genius are eager to begin an age of adventure, an age which will benefit all the people on this good earth.''[51]

May 18   United States launches *Apollo 10*.

July 16   United States launches *Apollo 11*.

July 20   U.S. astronauts Neil Armstrong and Buzz Aldrin land and walk on the moon. Nixon converses with them via telephone: ''Because of what you have done the heavens have become a part of man's world, and as you talk to us from the Sea of Tranquility, it inspires us to redouble our efforts to bring peace and tranquility to earth. For one priceless moment in the whole history of man all the people on this earth are truly one—one in their pride in what you have done and one in our prayers that you will return safely to earth.''[52]

July 22   NASA gets the go-ahead to proceed with *Skylab*, known as the Apollo Applications Program.

July 31   U.S. space probe *Mariner 6* sends back detailed pictures of Mars.

Aug. 5   U.S. space probe *Mariner 7* sends back detailed pictures of Mars.

Sept. 15   Nixon's Space Task Group releases its report, *The Post-Apollo Space Program: Directions for the Future.* It calls for a manned flight to Mars by the end of the century and an ambitious program of unmanned exploration as well.[53]

Nov. 14   United States launches *Apollo 12.*

1970

Mar. 7   Nixon releases his first policy statement concerning the future of the U.S. Space Program. "We must see our space effort, then, not only as an adventure of today but also as an investment in tomorrow."[54]

Apr. 11   United States launches *Apollo 13.* The mission runs into trouble. Nixon talks about the "perils of space."

Nov. 10   Soviet Union launches *Luna 17,* which contains the first robot moon rover, *Lunokhod 1.*

1971

Jan. 31   U.S. launches *Apollo 14.* Nixon compares the American people to "the people who must have stood on the dock at Palos, Spain, and watched Columbus' ships disappear, believing they were watching the end of a great event, when they were watching the beginning."[55]

Apr. 19   Soviet Union launches the first space station, *Salyut 1.*

July 26   United States launches *Apollo 15.* Of the moon mission, Nixon states, "Even as it reflects man's restless quest for his own future, so it also reenacts another of the 'deeper rituals of his bones'—not only the compulsion of the human spirit to know where we are going but the primal need in man's blood to know from what we have come."[56]

Nov. 13   U.S. space probe *Mariner 9* becomes the first artificial satellite of Mars.

1972

Jan. 5   Nixon authorizes the development of the Space Transportation System (STS), commonly known as the shuttle. He states that the shuttle will "transform the space frontier of the 1970s into familiar territory, easily accessible for human endeavor in the 1980's and 1990's."[57]

Apr. 16   United States launches *Apollo 16.*

May 2   United States launches Jupiter space probe *Pioneer 10.*

July 23   United States launches the Earth Resources Technology Satellite (*ERTS-1*, later *Landsat 1*), which will make the first comprehensive satellite mapping of the earth.

Dec. 7   United States launches *Apollo 17.*

Dec. 19   Nixon defends his space policy: "We are taking another long step in man's ancient search for his own beginnings, pressing beyond knowledge of the means of human existence to find, perhaps, the meaning of human existence. . . . The making of space history will continue, and this Nation means to play a major role in its making."[58]

1973

Apr. 5   United States launches space probe *Pioneer II.*

May 14   United States launches its experimental space laboratory, *Skylab.*

May 25   United States launches first *Skylab* crew to the space laboratory. Astronauts Pete Conrad, Joe Kerwin, and Paul Weitz stay aboard for twenty-eight days.

July 28   United States launches second *Skylab* crew. Astronauts Al Bean, Jack Lousma, and Owen Garriott stay aboard for fifty-nine days.

Oct. 10   U.S. vice president Spiro Agnew resigns. Gerald Ford's name is submitted as replacement.

Nov. 16   United States launches third and final *Skylab* crew.

Astronauts Jerry Carr, Ed Gibson, and Bill Pogue stay aboard for eighty-four days.

1974

Mar. 29   U.S. space probe *Mariner 10* takes close-up shots of Mercury.

May 17   The first U.S. geostationary weather satellite, *SMS-1*, reaches orbit.

July 13   In honor of the fifth anniversary of the first lunar landing, Nixon proclaims July 16-24, 1974, as National Space Week.[59]

Aug. 10   In the wake of the Watergate break-in and cover-up, Richard Nixon resigns. Gerald Ford takes the presidential oath.

Sept. 7   Ford comments on the upcoming space "hook-up" between the Soviet *Soyuz* and the United States *Apollo* space capsules: "I think all of us agree that the broader we can make our relationships in health, in environment, in space, and many other areas, the better it is for us."[60]

Nov. 4   Ford receives a crystal grown aboard the *Skylab* experimental space lab. "Most of us become so involved in trying to find solutions to the serious problems that we face today that we sometimes lose sight of the developments that hold promise for a better tomorrow. [This crystal] is a reminder that we should raise our sights to the broadening horizon available to us through our national investments in science and technology."[61]

1975

Apr. 11   Ford presents the Robert H. Goddard Memorial Trophy to the *Skylab* astronauts. He states that "the United States has achieved a great role in space," and emphasizes that he is "a complete believer in the accomplishments, the mission of a good, fine, forward-looking, visionary space program for America."[62]

July 15   A U.S. *Apollo* spacecraft links up with a Soviet *Soyuz* spacecraft in the first international manned space flight.

July 24   Ford congratulates the astronauts involved in the *Apollo-Soyuz* test program. "This has opened a new era of international cooperation," which will hopefully "provide all of us with an example to remember for many, many years to come."[63]

1976

Mar. 13   Ford addresses the space program in a Q&A session in Wilkesboro, North Carolina. He states that the space program "has had a great many benefits in agriculture, in weather, in scientific achievements," and expresses the belief that "it will maintain its present momentum and [continue to] give us the benefits in science, in agriculture, in weather, and all of the other things."[64]

May 4   U.S. launches *Lageos*, a laser-reflecting satellite that will investigate earth shape and crustal movements.

July 20   U.S. space probe *Viking I* lands on Mars.

Sept. 3   U.S. space probe *Viking II* lands on Mars.

Nov. 2   James Earl Carter is elected president of the United States.

1977

July 11   Carter proclaims July 16-24, 1977, as United States Space Observance Week. "The purpose of our space program is not only to study space, but to understand its relevance to life on earth."[65]

Aug. 12   U.S. prototype space shuttle orbiter *Enterprise* makes the first free flight from a Boeing 747 carrier aircraft. Also, the U.S. launches the first high-energy astronomy satellite, *HEAO-1*, to map X-ray and gamma-ray sources in the heavens.

Aug. 20   United States launches deep space probe *Voyager 2*.

Sept. 5   United States launches deep space probe *Voyager 1* in a faster trajectory than Voyager 2.

Oct. 26   U.S. prototype space shuttle orbiter *Enterprise* makes final approach and landing test.

Nov. 22   European Space Agency (ESA) launches a geostationary weather satellite, *Meteosat I.*

1978

Jan. 26   United States, in cooperation with the European Space Agency, launches an international ultraviolet explorer (IUE) that will record outer space at ultraviolet wavelengths.

May 20   United States launches interplanetary probe *Pioneer-Venus I.*

June 20   Carter calls for a total review of U.S. space activities. His directive "recognizes that the civilian space program is at the threshold of change," and he believes that "at issue is how to best capitalize on prior investments and set the needed direction and purpose for continued vitality in the future."[66]

July 20   Carter comments on the ninth anniversary of the first moon landing. He calls it "a moment without precedent in human experience," and then directs attention to the space shuttle, which will allow the United States "to use the vantage point of space to learn more about the Earth."[67]

Aug. 8   United States launches space probe *Pioneer-Venus 2.*

Oct. 1   Carter presides at the Congressional Space Medal of Honor awards ceremony. He states that the space age has "reached the threshold of its maturity," that "the first great era of the space age is over," and that "the second is about to begin."[68]

1979

Mar. 5   U.S. space probe *Voyager 1* makes its closest approach to Jupiter, sending back a wealth of information.

Mar. 27   Carter lays out his national space policy, which "stresses the use of space technologies to meet human needs here on earth."[69]

May 1   U.S. prototype orbiter *Enterprise* rolls out to the launch pad at Kennedy Space Center.

July 9   U.S. space probe *Voyager 2* does a fly-by of Jupiter.

July 11   U.S. space lab *Skylab* falls to earth, as planned, in western Australia.

July 17   Carter proclaims July 17-24 as United States Space Observance Week. "Ten years ago this week, the *Apollo* astronauts changed forever, for all humanity, our concept of the universe and our relation to it. . . . During the ten years since, space has become part of our daily lives."[70]

July 20   Ten-year anniversary of the *Apollo 11* moon landing. Carter says, "The pioneer spirit that built our great country is symbolized by the footprints of American astronauts on the bleak landscape of the Moon."[71]

Sept. 1   U.S. space probe *Pioneer 11* becomes the first probe to travel to Saturn.

Sept. 20   U.S. launches high-energy astronomical observatory *HEAO-3 (Einstein)* to explore the heavens at X-ray wavelengths.

Oct. 13   Carter reiterates his space policy during a telephone call-out program on National Public Radio: "We're moving into a new era of the use of space that will be quite different from what we've known in the past. . . . Now we are shifting to a more routine use of space flights with the shuttle."[72]

1980

Feb. 14   U.S. launches solar maximum mission satellite *Solar Max.*

Nov. 4   Ronald Reagan is elected president of the United States.

Nov. 12   U.S. space probe *Voyager 1* reaches Saturn and sends back pictures.

Dec. 6   United States launches *Intelsat V.* With 12,000 voice circuits, it is the first in a series of powerful communications satellites.

Dec. 29   United States rolls shuttle orbiter *Columbia* onto the launch pad.

1981

Apr. 12   United States launches maiden test flight of shuttle orbiter *Columbia*. Reagan says, "Through you, today, we all feel as giants once again."[73]

Aug. 25   U.S. space probe *Voyager 1* makes its closest approach to Saturn.

Nov. 12   United States launches shuttle orbiter *Columbia*. It is the first time any spacecraft has returned to space.

1982

Mar. 22   United States launches shuttle orbiter *Columbia*. The crew conducts scientific experiments.

Mar. 31   Reagan comments to the press about the shuttle: "With the successful completion of the *Columbia* space shuttle's latest mission, I think we were all reminded of the great things the human race can achieve when it harnesses its best minds and efforts to a positive goal."[74]

Apr. 19   Soviet Union launches space station *Salyut 7*.

June 27   United States launches shuttle orbiter *Columbia*. Reagan calls it "the historical equivalent to the driving of the golden spike which completed the first transcontinental railroad."[75]

July 4   Reagan presides over an Independence Day gathering of NASA officials at Edwards Air Force Base. He proclaims that the United States should work toward achieving a "real presence" in space.[76]

Nov. 11   United States launches shuttle orbiter *Columbia*, which launches two communications satellites.

1983

Mar. 23   Reagan announces plans for a Strategic Defensive Initiative (SDI), dubbed "Star Wars" by the press.

Apr. 4   United States launches maiden flight of shuttle orbiter *Challenger*, which deploys the first tracking and data relay satellite. Reagan states: "You and your ground crew are daring the future and the old ways of thinking that kept us looking to the heavens rather than traveling to them. You symbolize just how high America's hopes can soar."[77]

May 16   Reagan announces support for private-sector investment and involvement in civil space activities.[78]

June 18   United States launches shuttle orbiter *Challenger* and with it, the first U.S. female astronaut, Sally Ride. In his weekly radio address, Reagan acknowledges the seventh shuttle flight.[79]

Aug. 30   United States launches shuttle orbiter *Challenger*. The crew conducts scientific experiments.

Oct. 19   Reagan commends NASA on its twenty-fifth anniversary for engaging in an activity "fundamental to the American character: blazing the trail to an exciting new frontier."[80]

Nov. 28   United States launches shuttle orbiter *Columbia*. The crew conducts over seventy experiments. At the conclusion of the flight ten days later, Reagan states: "Your great success is a shining example of what free people working together can do. . . . New horizons have been discovered and old boundaries pushed back."[81]

1984

Jan. 25   Reagan directs NASA "to develop a permanently manned space station and to do it within a decade."[82]

Jan. 28   Reagan defends his space station directive, calling it "a doorway to even greater progress in the future."[83]

Feb. 3   United States launches shuttle orbiter *Challenger*, which deploys two communications satellites. Reagan sends his congratulations: "You're doing a fine job. Your commitment and courage on this historical flight, I think, are an inspiration to all of us."[84]

Mar. 1   U.S. earth-resources satellite (ERTS) *Landsat 5* ascends into orbit.

Apr. 6   United States launches shuttle orbiter *Challenger*, which deploys the long duration exposure facility (LDEF) and captures and repairs the *Solar Max* satellite. Reagan states: "We are very proud of what you're doing up there and what the future bodes for all of us with regard to this opening up of that great frontier of space."[85]

July 20   Reagan proclaims July 20, 1984, as Space Exploration Day 1984: "It is said there are two fundamental differences between human beings and other species: we have souls and we have curiosity. The exploration of space is a testament to each of these differences. It is our curiosity which drives our explorations, and it is our soul which gives these explorations meaning."[86]

July 20   Reagan comments on the fifteenth anniversary of the *Apollo 11* lunar landing: "Our freedom and well-being are tied to new achievements and pushing back new frontiers. We'll push back those frontiers and open new doors to discovery, opportunity, and progress."[87]

July 21   Reagan announces commercial space initiatives: "Now we're ready to make the desert bloom."[88]

Aug. 27   Reagan directs NASA to begin a search for candidates for the Teacher in Space Project.[89]

Aug. 30   United States launches maiden flight of shuttle orbiter *Discovery*, which deploys three communications satellites. Reagan states: "Yours is the work of a true revolution; not a revolution poisoned by hatred and violence and the will to conquer, but one that's rising from the deepest yearnings of the human spirit that challenge the limits of knowledge and [put] the power of discovery at the service of our most noble and generous impulses for decency, progress, and yes, for peace."[90]

Oct. 5   United States launches shuttle orbiter *Challenger*. The crew conducts experiments.

Oct. 17   Reagan launches the Young Astronaut Program:

"We won't be held back. We'll keep battling for the future, for new jobs and markets, for discovery, and for knowledge. We have a commitment to keep to our young poeple, our young astronauts, and we won't let them down."[91]

Nov. 8   United States launches shuttle orbiter *Discovery*, which deploys two satellites and retrieves two others.

1985

Jan. 24   United States launches shuttle orbiter *Discovery*, which carries a classified defense mission.

Apr. 12   United States launches shuttle orbiter *Discovery*, which deploys a communications satellite. Reagan congratulates: "I want you to know that we're rooting for you all. We saw a lot of human ingenuity at work."[92]

Apr. 29   United States launches shuttle orbiter *Challenger*. The crew conducts scientific experiments.

June 17   United States launches shuttle orbiter *Discovery*, which deploys a Saudi satellite, *Arabsat*.

June 26   Reagan comments on the finalists in the Teacher in Space Project. He calls teachers the "preservers and protectors of our heritage" who "save our past from being consumed by forgetfulness and our future from being engulfed in ignorance."[93]

July 20   Reagan proclaims July 20, 1985, as Space Exploration Day.

July 29   United States launches shuttle orbiter *Challenger*, which carries *Spacelab 2*.

Aug. 24   United States launches shuttle orbiter *Discovery*, which captures and repairs a malfunctioning satellite.

Oct. 3   United States launches maiden flight of shuttle orbiter *Atlantis*, which carries a classified defense mission.

Oct. 30   United States launches shuttle orbiter *Challenger*, which carries a West German space lab.

Nov. 26   United States launches shuttle orbiter *Atlantis*, which deploys three communications satellites.

1986

Jan. 12   United States launches shuttle orbiter *Columbia*. Scientific experiments are conducted.

Jan. 24   U.S. space probe *Voyager 2* sends back spectacular images of Uranus.

Jan. 28   U.S. shuttle orbiter *Challenger* explodes seventy-three seconds after liftoff. Seven astronants, including Commander Francis R. Scobee and crew members Michael J. Smith, Judith A. Resnik, Ronald E. McNair, Ellison S. Onizuka, Gregory B. Jarvis, and Sharon Christa McAuliffe, were killed. In an exchange with news reporters, Reagan states: "The world is a hazardous place, always has been. In pioneering we've always known that there are pioneers that give their lives out there on the frontier."[94] In his address to the nation that evening, Reagan states: "We've grown used to the idea of space, and perhaps we forget that we've only just begun. We're still pioneers."[95]

Jan. 29   Shuttle fleet grounded.

Feb. 3   Reagan commissions an investigation into the space shuttle *Challenger* accident.[96]

Feb. 19   Soviet Union launches *Mir*, a new modular space station with six docking ports.

Apr. 18   U.S. Titan 34D Air Force rocket carrying a Big Bird spy satellite blows up just after leaving the launch pad.

May 3   U.S. Delta 3914 launch vehicle malfunctions and has to be destroyed seventy-one seconds after liftoff.

May 12   Reagan swears in a new NASA administrator. "We need a steady hand on the tiller. These past few months have been a stormy period for NASA and the space program of the United States."[97]

June 9   Reagan receives the final report of the presidential commission investigating the space shuttle *Challenger* accident. "As we push forward in our conquest of space—and push forward we will—our shuttle program will be safer and better prepared for the challenges that lie ahead."[98]

Aug. 15   Reagan announces new policy for the space program. He commits to the building of a fourth shuttle orbiter, but turns the launching of private (nongovernment) satellites over to private industry. "The private sector, with its ingenuity and cost effectiveness, will be playing an increasingly important role in the American space effort."[99]

Sept. 5   U.S. Delta vehicle successfully launches a Strategic Defense Initiative payload.

Oct. 3   NASA announces February 1988 as the target date for resuming shuttle flights.[100]

1987

Jan. 28   Reagan comments on the first anniversary of the explosion of the space shuttle *Challenger*. Reagan reminds the country that "exploration has its risks" and reiterates his commitment to the space station, "our gateway to the universe, our foothold in outer space, the keystone of our space program. With it as our base camp, we will be able to reach the planets and, perhaps one day, to the stars."[101]

Dec. 1   NASA selects Boeing, McDonnell Douglas, General Electric, and Rockwell to design the permanently manned space station.

Dec. 23   The redesigned shuttle solid rocket booster is introduced by Morton Thiokol.

1988

Jan. 25   Reagan announces his space policy initiative. It includes "(1) promoting a strong commercial presence in space, . . . (2) assuring a highway to space by building on my previous efforts to promote a strong private expendable launch vehicle industry, and (3) building a solid technology and talent base."[102]

Sept. 29   United States finally launches shuttle orbiter *Discovery*. "American is back in space," Reagan assures the public, and adds, "I think I had my fingers crossed like everybody else."[103]

Nov. 6   George Bush is elected president of the United States.

Nov. 17   United States launches shuttle orbiter *Atlantis*, which carries a classified defense mission.

1989

Feb. 18   United States launches shuttle orbiter *Discovery*, which deploys a tracking and data relay satellite for NASA.

Apr. 29   United States launches shuttle orbiter *Atlantis*, which launches U.S. space probe *Magellan*, destined for Venus.

July 1   United States launches shuttle orbiter *Columbia*, which carries a classified defense mission.

July 20   Bush proposes that the United States should make the planned space station *Freedom* "the first step" in a "long range continuing commitment to manned exploration of the solar system." He directs his National Space Council to draw up "as soon as possible, a plan for establishing a base on the moon and sending astronauts to Mars."[104]

Aug. 10   United States launches shuttle orbiter *Discovery*, which carries a classified defense mission.

Oct. 12   United States launches shuttle orbiter *Atlantis*, which sends U.S. space probe *Galileo* to Jupiter.

Nov. 13   United States launches shuttle orbiter *Columbia*, which deploys one communications satellite.

Nov. 18   With its last unmanned rocket, United States launches the *Cosmic Background Explorer* spacecraft to study how stars and galaxies evolved from the "big bang."

Dec. 11   United States launches shuttle orbiter *Discovery*, which carries a classified defense mission.

1990

Jan. 9   United States launches shuttle orbiter *Columbia,* which rescues the long duration exposure facility.

Apr. 24   United States launches shuttle orbiter *Discovery,* which deploys the Hubble telescope.

Oct. 6   After a five-month launch hiatus due to mechanical failures and hydrogen leaks, the United States launches shuttle orbiter *Discovery.* It deploys space probe *Ulysses* on a mission to explore the polar regions of the sun.

Dec. 6   United States launches shuttle orbiter *Columbia.* Observation of celestial objects is conducted.

Dec. 11   Bush's Space Council releases its report, "The Future of the U.S. Space Program." The report argues that NASA should (1) move away from the shuttle and toward alternative expendable rockets; (2) redesign the proposed space station to make it cheaper and simpler, and more focused on the study of life in space; and (3) slow manned exploration of Mars to a "go as you pay" approach.[105]

NOTES

1. Dwight D. Eisenhower, "News Conference," 9 Oct. 1957, *Public Papers of the Presidents of the United States, Dwight D. Eisenhower, 1957* (Washington, D.C.: U.S. Government Printing Office, 1958), 720. (Hereafter abbreviated, *PPP, DDE, year.*)

2. Dwight D. Eisenhower, "Radio and Television Address to the American People on Science in National Security," 7 Nov. 1957, *PPP, DDE, 1957,* 798.

3. Dwight D. Eisenhower, 'Statement by the President Announcing the Successful Launching Into Orbit of an Earth Satellite,'" 1 Feb. 1958, *PPP, DDE, 1958* (Washington, D.C.: U.S. Government Printing Office, 1959), 141.

4. Dwight D. Eisenhower, "Statement by the President on Releasing the Science Advisory Committee's "Introduction to Outer Space," 26 Mar. 1958, *PPP, DDE, 1958,* 242-43.

5. Dwight D. Eisenhower, "Special Message to the Congress Relative to Space Science and Exploration," 2 April 1958, *PPP, DDE, 1958,* 270.

6. Dwight D. Eisenhower, "Statement by the President Upon Signing the National Aeronautics and Space Act of 1958," 29 July 1958," *PPP, DDE, 1958*, 573

7. Dwight D. Eisenhower, "News Conference," 28 Jan. 1959, *PPP, DDE, 1959* (Washington, D.C.: U.S. Government Printing Office, 1960), 137.

8. Dwight D. Eisenhower, "Letter to T. Keith Glennan, Administrator, National Aeronautics and Space Administration, Following the Launching of Space Probe Pioneer IV," 3 Mar. 1959, *PPP, DDE, 1959*, 224.

9. Dwight D. Eisenhower, "News Conference," 3 Aug. 1959, *PPP, DDE, 1959*, 555.

10. Dwight D. Eisenhower, "Statement by the President on the Proposed Transfer of the Army Ballistic Missiles Agency to the National Aeronautics and Space Administration," 21 Oct. 1959, *PPP, DDE, 1959*, 731.

11. Dwight D. Eisenhower, "News Conference," 22 Oct. 1959, *PPP, DDE, 1959*, 734.

12. Dwight D. Eisenhower, "News Conference," 26 Jan. 1960, *PPP, DDE, 1960-61* (Washington, D.C.: U.S. Government Printing Office, 1961), 127.

13. Dwight D. Eisenhower, "News Conference," 3 Feb. 1960, *PPP, DDE, 1960-61*, 145, 146.

14. Dwight D. Eisenhower, "Statement by the President on the Launching of Satellite Tiros I," 1 Apr. 1960, *PPP, DDE, 1960-61*, 330.

15. Dwight D. Eisenhower, "Remarks Upon Inspection of the Capsule Retrieved from the Satellite Discoverer XIII," 15 Aug. 1960, *PPP, DDE, 1960-61*, 632.

16. Dwight D. Eisenhower, "Statement by the President on the US Achievements in Space," 17 Aug. 1960, *PPP, DDE, 1960-61*, 643.

17. John F. Kennedy, "News Conference," 15 Feb. 1961, *Public Papers of the Presidents of the United States, John F. Kennedy, 1961* (Washington, D.C.: U.S. Government Printing Office, 1962), 95. (Hereafter *PPP, JFK, year*).

18. John F. Kennedy, "News Conference," 12 Apr. 1961, *PPP, JFK, 1961*, 263.

19. John F. Kennedy, "Statement by the President Upon Signing Bill Amending the Aeronautics and Space Act," 15 Apr. 1961, *PPP, JFK, 1961*, 321-22.

20. John F. Kennedy, "News Conference," 5 May 1961, *PPP, JFK, 1961*, 358.

21. John F. Kennedy, "Special Message to the Congress on Urgent National Needs," 25 May 1961, *PPP, JFK, 1961*, 403.

22. John F. Kennedy, "Address in Los Angeles at a Dinner of the Democratic Party of California," 18 Nov. 1961, *PPP, JFK, 1961,* 734.

23. John F. Kennedy, "News Conference," 21 Feb. 1962, *PPP, JFK, 1962* (Washington, D.C.: U.S. Government Printing Office, 1963), 151, 152.

24. John F. Kennedy, "Address at Rice University in Houston on the Nation's Space Effort," 12 Sept. 1962, *PPP, JFK, 1962,* 669.

25. John F. Kennedy, "Radio and Television Remarks Following the Flight of Astronaut L. Gordon Cooper," 16 May 1963, *PPP, JFK, 1963* (Washington, D.C.: U.S. Government Printing Office, 1964), 405.

26. John F. Kennedy, "Remarks Upon Presenting the Collier Trophy to the First U.S. Astronauts," 10 Oct. 1963, *PPP, JFK, 1963,* 775.

27. Lyndon B. Johnson, "Annual Message to the Congress on the State of the Union," 8 Jan. 1964, *Public Papers of the Presidents of the United States, Lyndon B. Johnson, 1963-64,* vol. I (Washington, D.C.: U.S. Government Printing Office, 1965), 117. (Hereafter *PPP, LBJ, year*).

28. Lyndon B. Johnson, "Statement by the President Following the Launching of the First Satellite by Saturn I," 29 Jan. 1964, *PPP, LBJ, 1963-64,* I:248.

29. Lyndon B. Johnson, "Remarks Upon Arrival at Edwards Air Force Base, California," 19 June 1964, *PPP, LBJ, 1963-64,* vol. II (Washington, D.C.: U.S. Government Printing Office, 1965), 782.

30. Lyndon B. Johnson, "Remarks After Inspecting Space Facilities at Cape Kennedy," 15 Sept. 1964, *PPP, LBJ, 1963-64,* II:1071.

31. Lyndon B. Johnson, "Remarks Following a Briefing at the National Aeronautics and Space Administration," 25 Feb. 1965, *PPP, LBJ, 1965,* vol. I (Washington, D.C.: U.S. Government Printing Office, 1966), 215.

32. Lyndon B. Johnson, "President's News Conference at the LBJ Ranch," 20 Mar. 1965, *PPP, LBJ, 1965,* I:306.

33. Lyndon B. Johnson, "Statement by the President on the Flight of Gemini 3," 23 Mar. 1965, *PPP, LBJ, 1965,* I:310.

34. Lyndon B. Johnson, "Telephone Conversation Between the President and Astronauts James McDivitt and Edward White," 7 June 1965, *PPP, LBJ, 1965,* vol. II (Washington, D.C.: U.S. Government Printing Office, 1966), 646.

35. Lyndon B. Johnson, "Remarks Upon Viewing New Mariner 4 Pictures From Mars," 29 July 1965, *PPP, LBJ, 1965,* II:806.

36. Lyndon B. Johnson, "Remarks by Telephone to Astronauts Cooper and Conrad Following Completion of the Gemini 5 Mission," 29 Aug. 1965, *PPP, LBJ, 1965,* II:942.

37. Lyndon B. Johnson, "Statement by the President on the Flight of Gemini 7," 4 Dec. 1965, *PPP, LBJ, 1965,* II:1135.

38. Lyndon B. Johnson, "Telegram to the Administrator, NASA, Following the Meeting in Space of Gemini 6 and Gemini 7," 15 Dec. 1965, *PPP, LBJ, 1965,* II:1156-57.

39. Lyndon B. Johnson, "Remarks Upon Accepting the Robert H. Goddard Trophy," 16 Mar. 1966, *PPP, LBJ, 1966,* vol. I (Washington, D.C.: U.S. Government Printing Office, 1967), 330.

40. Lyndon B. Johnson, "Statement by the President on the Need for a Treaty Governing Exploration of Celestial Bodies," 7 May 1966, *PPP, LBJ, 1966,* I:487.

41. Lyndon B. Johnson, "Statement by the President Following the Landing of Surveyor I on the Moon," 2 June 1966," *PPP, LBJ, 1966,* I:575.

42. Lyndon B. Johnson, "Remarks at an Award Ceremony at the LBJ Ranch Marking the Conclusion of the Gemini Space Program," 23 Nov. 1966, *PPP, LBJ, 1966,* vol. II (Washington, D.C.: U.S. Government Printing Office, 1967), 1396.

43. Lyndon B. Johnson, "Statement by the President on the Death of Astronauts Virgil I. Grissom, Edward H. White 2d, and Roger B. Chaffee," 27 Jan. 1967, *PPP, LBJ, 1967,* vol. I (Washington, D.C.: U.S. Government Printing Office, 1968), 92.

44. Lyndon B. Johnson, "Remarks at the Signing of the Treaty on Outer Space," 27 Jan. 1967, *PPP, LBJ, 1967,* I:91.

45. Lyndon B. Johnson, "Remarks at Ceremony Marking the Entry Into Force of the Outer Space Treaty," 10 Oct. 1967, *PPP, LBJ, 1967,* vol. II (Washington, D.C.: U.S. Government Printing Office, 1968), 919.

46. Lyndon B. Johnson, "Special Message to the Senate on the Astronaut Assistance and Return Agreement," 15 July 1968, *PPP, LBJ, 1968-69,* vol. II (Washington, D.C.: U.S. Government Printing Office, 1970), 809.

47. Lyndon B. Johnson, "Statement by the President on the 10th Anniversary of the National Aeronautics and Space Administration," 1 Oct. 1968, *PPP, LBJ, 1968-69,* II:998.

48. Lyndon B. Johnson, "Message to the Apollo 7 Astronauts," 11 Oct. 1968, *PPP, LBJ, 1968-69,* II:1032.

49. Lyndon B. Johnson, "Message to the Apollo 8 Astronauts at the Beginning of their Flight to the Moon." 21 Dec. 1968, *PPP, LBJ, 1968-69,* II:1208.

50. Richard M. Nixon, quoted in Howard E. McCurdy, *The Space Station Decision: Incremental Politics and Technological Choice* (Baltimore: Johns Hopkins University Press, 1990), 23.

51. Richard M. Nixon, "Telegram to the Crew of Apollo 9," 13 Mar. 1969, *Public Papers of the Presidents of the United States, Richard M. Nixon,*

1969 (Washington: D.C.: U.S. Government Printing Office, 1971), 207-8. (Hereafter *PPP, RMN, year*).

52. Richard M. Nixon, "Telephone Conversation with the Apollo 11 Astronauts on the Moon," 20 July 1969, *PPP, RMN, 1969*, 530.

53. Space Task Group, *The Post-Apollo Space Program: Directions for the Future*, Report to the President (Washington, D.C.: Executive Office of the President, September 1969).

54. Richard M. Nixon, "Statement About the Future of the United States Space Program," 7 Mar. 1970, *PPP, RMN, 1970* (Washington, D.C.: U.S. Government Printing Office, 1971), 251.

55. Richard M. Nixon, "Statement Following the Successful Launch of Apollo 14," 31 Jan. 1971, *PPP, RMN, 1971* (Washington, D.C.: U.S. Government Printing Office, 1972), 97.

56. Richard M. Nixon, "Statement Following the Successful Launch of Apollo 15," 26 July 1971, *PPP, RMN, 1971*, 826.

57. Richard M. Nixon, "Statement Announcing Decision to Proceed with Development of the Space Shuttle," 5 Jan. 1972, *PPP, RMN, 1972* (Washington, D.C.: U.S. Government Printing Office, 1974), 20.

58. Richard M. Nixon, "Statement About the Space Program," 19 Dec. 1972, *PPP, RMN, 1972*, 1157, 1158.

59. Richard M. Nixon, "Exchange of Remarks with Former Astronaut Neil A. Armstrong about United States Space Week," *PPP, RMN, 1974* (Washington, D.C.: U.S. Government Printing Office, 1976), 598-99.

60. Gerald R. Ford, "Remarks at the Alexandria Police Association Picnic in Fairfax, Virginia," 7 Sept. 1974, *Public Papers of the Presidents of the United States, Gerald R. Ford, 1974* (Washington, D.C.: U.S. Government Printing Office, 1975), 99. (Hereafter *PPP, GRF, year*.)

61. Gerald R. Ford, "Statement on Receiving a Crystal Grown Aboard the Skylab Space Station," 4 Nov. 1974, *PPP, GRF, 1974*, 577.

62. Gerald R. Ford, "Remarks Upon Presenting the Robert H. Goddard Memorial Trophy to the Skylab Astronauts," 11 April 1975, *PPP, GRF, 1975*, vol. I (Washington, D.C.: U.S. Government Printing Office, 1977), 473, 474.

63. Gerald R. Ford, "Telephone Conversation with the Astronauts of the Apollo-Soyuz Test Project Following Recovery of Their Spacecraft," 24 July 1975, *PPP, GRF, 1975*, vol. II (Washington, D.C.: U.S. Government Printing Office, 1977), 1029.

64. Gerald R. Ford, "Remarks and a Question and Answer Session in Wilkesboro, North Carolina," 13 Mar. 1976, *PPP, GRF, 1976-77* (Washington, D.C.: U.S. Government Printing Office, 1979), 706.

65. James E. Carter, "United States Space Observance, Proclamation

4512," 11 July 1977, *Public Papers of the Presidents of the United States, James Earl Carter, 1977,* vol. II (Washington, D.C.: U.S. Government Printing Office, 1978), 1227. (Hereafter *PPP, JEC, year*).

66. James E. Carter, "Announcement of Administration Review of United States Space Activities," 20 June 1978, *PPP, JEC, 1978,* vol. I (Washington, D.C.: U.S. Government Printing Office, 1979), 1135.

67. James E. Carter, "Statement by the President on the Ninth Anniversary of the First Moon Landing," 20 July 1978, *PPP, JEC, 1978,* vol. II (Washington, D.C.: U.S. Government Printing Office, 1979), 1322.

68. James E. Carter, "Remarks at the Congressional Space Medal of Honor Awards Ceremony, Kennedy Space Center, Florida," 1 Oct. 1978, *PPP, JEC, 1978,* II: 1685, 1686.

69. James E. Carter, "Message to Congress on Science & Technology," 27 Mar. 1979, *PPP, JEC, 1979,* vol. I (Washington, D.C.: U.S. Government Printing Office, 1980), 536.

70. James E. Carter, "Proclamation 46669, United States Space Observance, 1979," 17 July 1979, *PPP, JEC, 1979,* vol. II (Washington, D.C.: U.S. Government Printing Office, 1980), 1260.

71. James E. Carter, "Remarks at a Ceremony in Observance of the 10th Anniversary of the Moon Landing," 20 July 1979, *PPP, JEC, 1979,* II: 1276-77.

72. James E. Carter, "Ask the President, Remarks during a Telephone Call-Out Program on National Public Radio," 13 Oct. 1979, *PPP, JEC, 1979,* II: 1911.

73. Ronald Reagan, "Statement to the *Columbia* Astronauts on the Inaugural Flight of the Space Shuttle," 9 Apr. 1981, *Public Papers of the Presidents of the United States, Ronald Reagan, 1981* (Washington, D.C.: U.S. Government Printing Office, 1982), 348. (Hereafter, *PPP, RR, year*).

74. Ronald Reagan, "The President's News Conference," 31 Mar. 1982, *PPP, RR, 1982,* vol. I (Washington, D.C.: U.S. Government Printing Office, 1983), 399.

75. Ronald Reagan, "Remarks at Edwards Air Force Base, California, on Completion of the Fourth Mission of the Space Shuttle *Columbia*," 4 July 1982, *PPP, RR, 1982,* vol. II (Washington, D.C.: U.S. Government Printing Office, 1983), 892.

76. Ronald Reagan, "Remarks at Edwards Air Force Base," *PPP, RR, 1982,* II: 893.

77. Ronald Reagan, "Message to the Space Shuttle *Challenger* Astronauts," 4 Apr. 1983, *PPP, RR, 1983,* vol. I (Washington, D.C.: U.S. Government Printing Office, 1984), 490.

78. Ronald Reagan, "Announcement of United States Government

Support for Private Sector Commercial operations of Expendable Launch Vehicles,'' 16 May 1983, *PPP, RR, 1983,* I: 712-14.

79. Ronald Reagan, ''Radio Address to the Nation on the Federal Reserve Board Chairman, the Seventh Space Shuttle Flight, and Science Education,'' 18 June 1983, *PPP, RR, 1983,* I: 887.

80. Ronald Reagan, ''Remarks at the 25th Anniversary Celebration of the National Aeronautics and Space Administration,'' 19 Oct. 1983, *PPP, RR, 1983,* vol. II (Washington, D.C.: U.S. Government Printing Office, 1984), 1481.

81. Ronald Reagan, ''Statement on the Conclusion of the Space Shuttle *Columbia* Mission,'' 8 Dec. 1983, *PPP, RR, 1983,* II: 1672.

82. Ronald Reagan, ''Address Before a Joint Session of the Congress on the State of the Union,'' 25 Jan. 1984, *PPP, RR, 1984,* vol. I (Washington, D.C.: U.S. Government Printing Office, 1986), 90.

83. Ronald Reagan, ''Radio Address to the Nation on the Space Program,'' 28 Jan. 1984, *PPP, RR, 1984,* I: 108.

84. Ronald Reagan, ''Remarks by Telephone to Crewmembers on Board the Space Shuttle *Challenger*,'' 9 Feb. 1984, *PPP, RR, 1984,* I: 188.

85. Ronald Reagan, ''Remarks by Telephone with Crewmembers on Board the Space Shuttle *Challenger*,'' 10 Apr. 1984, *PPP, RR, 1984,* I: 500.

86. Ronald Reagan, ''Proclamation 5224-Space Exploration Day, 1984,'' 20 July 1984, *PPP, RR, 1984,* vol. II (Washington, D.C.: U.S. Government Printing Office, 1986), 1069.

87. Ronald Reagan, ''Remarks at a White House Ceremony Marking the 15th Anniversary of the Apollo 11 Lunar Landing,'' 20 July 1984, *PPP, RR, 1984,* II: 1067.

88. Ronald Reagan, ''Radio Address to the Nation on Commercial Space Initiatives,'' 21 July 1984, *PPP, RR, 1984,* II: 1071.

89. Ronald Reagan, ''Remarks at a Ceremony Honoring the 1983-84 Winners in the Secondary School Recognition Program,'' 27 Aug. 1984, *PPP, RR, 1984,* II: 1198

90. Ronald Reagan, ''Remarks During a Visit to the Goddard Space Flight Center in Greenbelt, Maryland,'' 30 Aug. 1984, *PPP, RR, 1984,* II: 1206.

91. Ronald Reagan, ''Remarks at a White House Ceremony Launching the Young Astronaut Program,'' 17 Oct. 1984, *PPP, RR, 1984,* II: 1565.

92. Ronald Reagan, ''Telephone Conversation with the Astronauts on Board the Space Shuttle *Discovery*,'' 18 Apr. 1985, *PPP, RR, 1985,* vol. I (Washington, D.C.: U.S. Government Printing Office, 1988), 449.

93. Ronald Reagan, ''Remarks to the Finalists in the Teacher in

Space Project," 26 June 1985, *PPP, RR, 1985*, I: 825.

94. Ronald Reagan, "Exchange with Reporters on the Explosion of the Space Shuttle *Challenger*," 28 Jan. 1986, *PPP, RR, 1986*), vol. I (Washington, D.C.: U.S. Government Printing Office, 1988), 94.

95. Ronald Reagan, "Address to the Nation on the Explosion of the Space Shuttle *Challenger*," 28 Jan. 1986, *PPP, RR, 1986*, I: 95.

96. Ronald Reagan, "Executive Order 12546-Presidential Commission on the Space Shuttle *Challenger* Accident," 3 Feb. 1986, *PPP, RR, 1986*, I: 117.

97. Ronald Reagan, "Remarks at the Swearing-in Ceremony for James C. Fletcher as Administrator of the National Aeronautics and Space Administration," 12 May 1986, *PPP, RR, 1986*, I: 582.

98. Ronald Reagan, "Remarks on Receiving the Final Report of the Presidential Commission on the Space Shuttle *Challenger* Accident," 9 June 1986, *PPP, RR, 1986*, I: 736.

99. Ronald Reagan, "Statement on the Building of a Fourth Shuttle Orbiter and the Future of the Space Program," 15 Aug. 1986, *PPP, RR, 1986*, vol. II (Washington, D.C.: U.S. Government Printing Office, 1988), 1111.

100. Robin Kerrod, *The Illustrated History of NASA* Anniversary Edition (New York: Gallery Books, 1986; Multimedia Publications (UK) Ltd. 1988.), 253.

101. Ronald Reagan, "Remarks to Employees of the National Aeronautics and Space Administration on the First Anniversary of the Explosion of the Space Shuttle *Challenger*," 28 Jan. 1987, *PPP, RR, 1987*, vol. I (Washington, D.C.: U.S. Government Printing Office, 1989), 79-80.

102. Ronald Reagan, "1988 Legislative and Administrative Message: A Union of Individuals," 25 Jan. 1988, *PPP, RR, 1988*, vol. I (Washington, D.C.: U.S. Government Printing Office, 1990), 119.

103. "The Magic is Back!" *Time* 10 Oct. 1988, 22.

104. Kathy Sawyer, "Bush Urges Commitment to New Space Exploration," *Washington Post* 21 July 1989, A4.

105. "Panel Says NASA Needs an Overhaul," *Minneapolis Star Tribune* 11 Dec. 1990, 1A.

Selected Bibliography

Allaway, Howard. *The Space Shuttle at Work.* Washington, D.C.: NASA, 1979.

Barber, James. *Choosing the President.* Englewood Cliffs, N.J.: Prentice Hall, 1974.

Bond, Peter. *Heroes in Space from Gagarin to Challenger.* New York: Basil Blackwell, 1987.

Brauer, Carl M. *Presidential Transitions: Eisenhower through Reagan.* New York: Oxford University Press, 1986.

Brooks, Courtney G., James M. Grimwood, and Lloyd S. Swenson, Jr. *Chariots for Apollo: A History of Manned Lunar Spacecraft.* Washington, D.C.: NASA, 1979.

Carter, Dale. *The Final Frontier: The Rise and Fall of the American Rocket State.* London: Verso, 1988.

Collins, Michael. *Liftoff: The Story of America's Adventure in Space.* New York: Grove Press, 1988.

Cox, Donald W. *The Space Race.* Philadelphia: Chilton Books, 1962.

Denton, Robert E., Jr. *The Symbolic Dimensions of the American Presidency: Description and Analysis.* Prospect Heights, Ill.: Waveland, 1982.

Diamond, Edwin. *The Rise and Fall of the Space Age.* Garden City, N.Y.: Doubleday, 1964.

Gardner, Robert. *Space, Frontier of the Future.* Garden City, N.Y.: Doubleday, 1980.

Grey, Jerry. *Beachheads in Space.* New York: Macmillan, 1983.

Haggerty, James J. *Spinoff 1978: An Annual Report (NASA).* Washington, D.C.: U.S. Government Printing Office, 1978.

_____. *Spinoff 1979: An Annual Report (NASA).* Washington, D.C.: U.S. Government Printing Office, 1979.

Hart, Roderick P. *The Sound of Leadership: Presidential Communication in the Modern Age*. Chicago: University of Chicago Press, 1987.

Hirsch, Lester M., ed. *Man and Space*. New York: Pitman, 1966.

Holmes, Jay. *America on the Moon: The Enterprise of the Sixties*. Philadelphia: Lippincott, 1962.

Kerrod, Robin. *The Illustrated History of NASA*. Anniversary Edition. New York: Gallery Books, 1988.

Lewis, Richard S. *Space in the 21st Century*. New York: Columbia University Press, 1990.

Lindaman, Edward B. *Space, a New Direction for Mankind*. New York: Harper, 1969.

McCurdy, Howard E. *The Space Station Decision*. Baltimore: Johns Hopkins University Press, 1990.

McDonough, Thomas R. *Space: The Next Twenty-Five Years* (rev. and updated). New York: John Wiley and Sons, 1987; rpt., 1989.

McDougall, Walter A. *. . . The Heavens and the Earth: A Political History of the Space Age*. New York: Basic Books, 1985.

Murray, Bruce. *Journey into Space: The First Thirty Years of Space Exploration*. New York: W. W. Norton, 1989.

Murray, Charles, and Catherine Bly Cox. *Apollo*. New York: Simon and Schuster, 1989.

Needell, Allan A., ed. *The First 25 Years in Space: A Symposium*. Washington, D.C.: The Smithsonian Institution, 1983.

Oberg, James E. *The New Race for Space*. Harrisburg, Pa.: Stackpole Books, 1984.

Office of the Federal Register, National Archives and Records Services. *Public Papers of the Presidents of the United States*. Washington, D.C.: U.S. Government Printing Office, 1957-1988.

Ride, Sally K. *Leadership on America's Future in Space*. Washington, D.C.: U.S. Government Printing Office, 1988.

Shelton, William Roy. *American Space Exploration: The First Decade*. Boston: Little, Brown, 1967.

Shipman, Harry L. *Humans in Space: 21st Century Frontiers*. New York: Plenum, 1989.

Stares, Paul B. *The Militarization of Space*. Ithaca, NY: Cornell University Press, 1985.

Tulis, Jeffrey K. *The Rhetorical Presidency*. Princeton, N.J.: Princeton University Press, 1987.

Zarefsky, David. *President Johnson's War on Poverty*. Tuscaloosa: University of Alabama Press, 1986.

Index

About the Author

LINDA T. KRUG is an Assistant Professor in the Department of Communication at the University of Minnesota-Duluth. Her interest is in metaphor, especially in the way in which metaphor works to open up, close down, and establish competing perspectives. This subject has also been the focus of a number of her essays and convention presentations.